C000253753

DISCOVERING
SOUTH YORKSHIRE

Discovering South Yorkshire

*Its Hidden Places, Curiosities and Strange Events
with Brian Elliott*

First published in 1998 by

Smith Settle Ltd
Ilkley Road
Otley
West Yorkshire
LS21 3JP

© Brian Elliott 1998

All rights reserved. No part of this book may be
reproduced, stored or introduced into a retrieval system,
or transmitted in any form or by any means (electronic,
mechanical, photocopying, recording or otherwise)
without the permission of Smith Settle Ltd.

The right of Brian Elliott to be identified as the
author of this work has been asserted by him in accordance
with the Copyright, Designs and Patents Act 1988.

ISBN 1 85825 092 7

British Library Cataloguing-in-Publication Data:
A catalogue record is available for this book
from the British Library.

Opening page: milestone near Bradfield
Title page: Cannon Hall

Set in Souvenir.

Designed, printed and bound by
SMITH SETTLE
Ilkley Road, Otley, West Yorkshire LS21 3JP

Contents

Round and About Rotherham

Barnsley and Beyond

In and Around Doncaster

Introduction

The modern county of South Yorkshire contains some of the most varied scenery in Britain. Westwards, the landscape changes from the moors and foothills of the Pennines to the flatlands of Hatfield and Thorne. The area not only has a great deal of character but a long, interesting history and many places of interest for both residents and visitors.

The main urban areas form the metropolitan boroughs of Barnsley, Rotherham, Doncaster and the City of Sheffield, offering an easy way to divide up this book into sections. By reference to 106 sites, the contents do no more than offer a flavour of such a diverse area. The choice has therefore been unashamedly based on my own interests and experiences rather than the product of a systematic survey, but this may have advantages in term of enthusiasm and wetting the reader's appetite for more examples.

However, there has been a conscious attempt in the selection of subjects to relate to some of the major developments that have transformed part of the older industrial areas of the county since its formation only thirteen years ago. Thus Meadowhall rightly appears, as part of the remarkable regeneration of the Lower Don Valley which has been transformed under the Sheffield Development Corporation. Old and new sites have also been chosen in the rapidly changing Dearne Valley, where collaboration, partnership and successful funding bids are breathing new life into the area. The transformation of the derelict Manvers site and the development of associated transport links has been an equally significant achievement. The immense impact of coalmining has deservedly been given some prominence, and the demise of mining communities such as Grimethorpe more than acknowledged. Although not covered in the book, the Earth Centre at Denaby Main is now scheduled to re-open in the spring of 1999 following a highly successful bid to the Millennium Fund. The rejuvenation of the county's oldest tourist site, Conisbrough Castle, developments at the Elsecar Discovery Centre, and the very successful opening of Brodsworth Hall, has brought new interest and pride in the area.

Unfortunately, important sites remain under serious threat because of funding problems. The announcement by Sheffield City Council, on April Fools Day 1997, that Abbeydale Industrial Hamlet was to be 'mothballed' because of financial cuts is certainly no joke to the many thousands of people who appreciate the value of understanding our industrial past.

All the sites are accessible by car or by a short, easy walk from a car. Some are on private property, so please respect the privacy of the owners. General location maps and brief directions have been provided to assist the reader, but the sites are best identified via the Landranger and Pathfinder Ordnance Survey maps. The reference numbers used in all the maps and the index refer to the page on which the particular item appears.

I would like to express special appreciation to Arthur Clayton and David Hey who, over many years, have done so much to help and encourage my interest in local history. For help with particular sites, my thanks are due to Alice Rodgers, Roger Glister, Elizabeth Beighton and, for photographs, Meadowhall Shopping and Leisure Centre, Hellaby Hall Hotel and Aston Hall Hotel, Professor F T Evans and Rotherham Archives. All other photographs are by the author. Thanks also to Mark Whitley and all involved in the production of the book at Smith Settle.

Brian Elliott
Warmsworth, Doncaster
January 1998

Overall Map of South Yorkshire

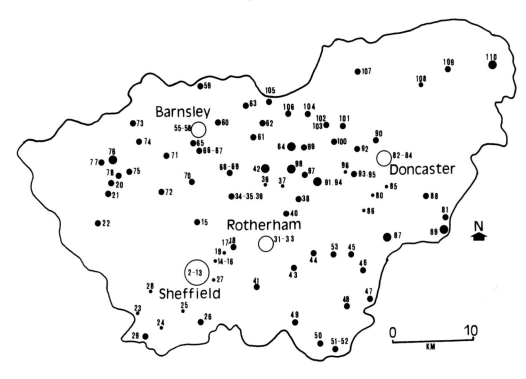

2	George Talbot's memorial	19	Carbrook Hall
3	Broadbent's House	20	Hollin Busk mine
4	Firth Court, Sheffield	21	Bolsterstone village
5	Elliott memorial	22	Bradfield Church watchtower
6	Mappin Art Gallery	23	Ringinglow tollhouse
7	Fire Museum	24	Abbeydale Industrial Hamlet
8	Old Queens Head	25	Bishops House Museum
9	Park Hill	26	Chantryland, Graves Park
10	Kelham Island Museum	27	Manor Lodge
11	cementation furnace	28	Shepherd Wheel
12	Green Lane Works	29	Dore village monuments
13	Globe Works	31	All Saints Church, Doncaster
14	Hill Top Chapel	32	Bridge Chapel, Doncaster
15	Ecclesfield Church	33	Clifton House and Park
16	Huntsman's memorial	34	Mechanics Institute, Wentworth
17	Meadowhall	35	Needle's Eye, Wentworth
18	teemers' statue, Meadowhall	36	Rockingham Pottery kiln

Sheffield and Hallamshire

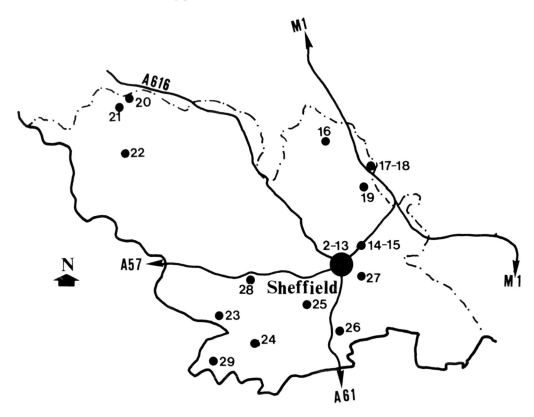

2	George Talbot's memorial
3	Broadbent's House
4	Firth Court, Sheffield
5	Elliott memorial
6	Mappin Art Gallery
7	Fire Museum
8	Old Queens Head
9	Park Hill
10	Kelham Island Museum
11	Sheffield's cementation furnace
12	Green Lane Works
13	Globe Works
14	Hill Top Chapel
16	Huntsman's memorial
15	Ecclesfield Church
18	teemers' statue, Meadowhall
17	Meadowhall
19	Carbrook Hall
20	Hollin Busk mine
21	Bolsterstone village
22	Bradfield Church watchtower
23	Ringinglow tollhouse
24	Abbeydale Industrial Hamlet
25	Bishops' House Museum
26	Chantryland, Graves Park
27	Manor Lodge
28	Shepherd Wheel
29	Dore village monuments

George Talbot's Memorial

Reaching nearly to the roof of the south wall of the south chapel of Sheffield Cathedral is the spectacular monument of George Talbot, the sixth earl of Shrewsbury, one of the wealthiest of the Elizabethan nobility. The lordship of Sheffield was Gilbert's most valuable estate and though his fortress home was the castle at the meeting of the Sheaf and Don, he preferred life at his hill-top residence of Manor Lodge *(see page 27)*.

His funeral was of suitable pomp and ceremony for someone of such high rank. On a bitter January night in 1591 the earl's cortège slowly advanced towards the

Shrewsbury Chapel in the parish church of St Peter and St Paul, the long, winding procession lead by two men carrying black staves, followed by 70 yeomen and grooms and 300 mourners. The Archbishop of York (who would have read the sermon) and his entourage was at the rear; and last the main family mourners including Lady Shrewsbury (Bess of Hardwick). It was claimed that 20,000 people were present, customary dole being given to the poorest 8,000. A similar ceremony marked the passing of the seventh earl, in 1616, but this was to be the last great Shrewsbury funeral in Sheffield.

Site: Shrewsbury Chapel, Sheffield Cathedral.

Grid Ref: SK 354876 (Landranger 110 or 111, Pathfinder 743)

Broadbent's House

To the north of the former parish church are the remains of the Georgian quarter of Sheffield. The address of one of the most interesting buildings is 3 Hartshead, also known as the Old Banker's House or Broadbent's House.

It is a handsome brick town-house of three storeys and five bays, with tall twelve-pane windows. The central part has an attractive narrow doorway and triangular pediment under an equally fine window. Stone pilasters, on either side of the entrance, rusticated from the first floor, extend beyond the cornice to roof level, emphasising the height of the structure. The house appears to have been built in 1728 for Nicholas and Rebecca Broadbent, the year and their initials on a rainwater head. From 1771 until 1782 it was used as a bank under the ownership of grandson Thomas Broadbent who was also responsible for developing nearby properties. Broadbent is alleged to have continued to accept deposits even after knowing about imminent closure. The failure understandably affected Broadbent's personal wealth, health and social standing. He was described as 'moving about, a pathetic object, bearing all the symbols of extreme poverty'.

Site: 3 Hartshead, near Sheffield Cathedral.

Grid Ref: SK 356876 (Landranger 110 or 111, Pathfinder 743)

The Birth of a University

In gleaming red brick, the original university building on Western Bank was designed by E Mitchel Gibbs in 1903-5, a spectacular composition in the Tudor style. An octagonal library (out of shot) was added to the left (Weston Park) end by the same architect in 1909-11.

The university evolved from three institutions: the Sheffield School of Medicine (Founded in 1828), Firth College (1879) and the Sheffield Technical School (1884). The campaign to amalgamate and obtain a university charter was summarised in a pamphlet that called for public support on the grounds that the new institution would be 'for the people'; would bring 'the highest education within the reach of the working man'; would 'help local industries'; and would be a centre for the study of the 'treatment of accidents and diseases'. Support was also said to be essential for the future of Sheffield, 'the only large city in England without a University' and for the benefit of the nation 'in its trade competition with other nations'. The relatively recent successful establishment of Sheffield Hallam University rightly confirms the city as a major place of learning and research for and well beyond the millennium.

Site: Western Bank, Sheffield.

Grid Ref: SK 342873 (Landranger 110 or 111, Pathfinder 743)

The 'Poor Man's Poet'

Appropriately funded by 'working men', the seated statue of Ebenezer Elliott (by N N Burnard, 1854), the 'Corn Law Rhymer' and 'Poor Man's Poet', which once graced the market place of Sheffield is located in Weston Park, inscribed with a single word. Born in 1787 at Masborough where his father had a foundry, Elliott made a successful living in the Sheffield iron trade, retiring to Great Houghton where he died in 1849 and was buried in Darfield churchyard *(see page 61)*. He was a virulent critic of the despised 'bread tax' which he condemned with great passion in *Corn Law Rhymes* (1831). His writings hammered so effectively at the national conscience in pieces such as *The Village Patriarch* (1829) and *The People's Anthem* (1847) that he was a household name. Elliott's

unashamed honesty lead to unfair accusations that he was a dangerous radical. But, as Ray Hearne has shown, he was 'his own man', fearful of nobody, believing that society could be changed for the better by peaceful means. Now almost a forgotten figure, Elliott deserves his rightful place amongst the great nineteenth century poets.

Site: near the south gate of Weston Park, Western Bank, Sheffield.

Grid Ref: SK 339874 (Landranger 110 or 111, Pathfinder 743)

Art for All

Designed in 1886-88, and built at a cost of £15,000, the Mappin Art Gallery is one of Sheffield's most impressive classical buildings, the Ionic composition chosen by architects Flockton and Gibbs notable for its long colonnaded front.

The gallery was founded under the terms of the will of wealthy cutlery entrepreneur John Newton Mappin who bequeathed 153 paintings. A nephew, Sir Frederick Mappin, who was a gallery trustee, presented a further 48 pictures at the grand opening. Today, visitors can enjoy a wide variety of paintings and regular exhibitions; and the Mappin Art Workshops provide creative opportunities for people of all ages and abilities. Not surprisingly, the adjoining City Museum, built in 1937, has the world's finest collection of cutlery.

Site: Weston Park, Sheffield. The museum is open Wed–Sat 10am–5pm, Sun 11am–5pm.
Grid Ref: SK 338874 (Landranger 110 or 111, Pathfinder 743)

Flying Hooves and Gleaming Helmets

When the West Bar Fire and Police Station opened in September 1900, horse-drawn engines were still in use but the design of the building ensured a rapid emergency exit. With hooves flying and helmets gleaming, what a spectacular sight it must have been. By 1907 response time was halved when motor-power was introduced.

The South York-shire Fire Services Historical Society, formed in 1982, secured a lease of the old station in 1984. On architectural grounds alone the attractive red brick building, empty for years, did not deserve abandonment and possible demolition. After a great deal of voluntary restoration work, part of the historic station was opened as a fire museum in 1985, and is now the largest example in Great Britain open to the public on a regular basis. The Fire

Museum has established a well-earned reputation, its fine collection of equipment, artefacts and archives attracting international interest and serving as an educational resource — a remarkable achievement for a small voluntary team.

Site: 101-109 West Bar, Sheffield. The Fire Museum is open to the public on Sundays between 11am and 5pm, and has a shop and cafeteria.

Grid Ref: SK 356877 (Landranger 110 or 111, Pathfinder 743)

'... the hawle in the Poandes'

The Ponds was the name of the large, flat and marshy area alongside the River Sheaf where man-made ponds provided a store of water to power the Lord of Manor's corn mill and fish for his table.

The 'hawle in the Poandes', as it was referred to in an inventory of 1582, now the Old Queens Head, is a most surprising survivor, totally surrounded by modern development. Although it is a two-bay remnant of a much larger original and has a modern slate roof, it is an extremely interesting timber-framed structure. Of particular note are a series of carved heads on corbels at the front of the house. It has a projecting upper storey which would also have contained jettied windows. It was probably built by the fourth earl of Shrewsbury, possibly as a convenient but high-status refreshment facility. Dendrochronological (tree-ring) samples indicate a felling date between 1503 and 1510 for some of the main timbers. It was let to tenants as a wash-house from the seventeenth century.

Site: Pond Hill, next to the Sheffield Transport Interchange.

Grid Ref: SK 358873 (Landranger 111, Pathfinder 743)

Streets in the Sky

The Park Hill housing complex dominates the eastern skyline of the city of Sheffield. The City Corporation Architect's Department was given the job of rehousing thousands of families in the late 1950s on a difficult and prominent site. Drawing on the ideas of the French Modernist pioneer, Le Corbusier, the answer was found in a variable-storeyed structure that wove its way around the contours of the hillside, maintaining a continuous-level skyline. Another most innovatory feature was the provision of ten-foot (3m) wide decks or landings — 'streets in the sky'.

Park Hill has attracted national and international interest from town planners and architects. Unlike the earlier, equally innovative and now demolished Quarry Hill Flats at Leeds, Park Hill appears to have a future despite all the criticism associated with high-rise housing, since it has been recommended for Grade II (star) listing by English Heritage.

Site: Park Hill, between Sheaf Street & Duke Street, Sheffield.

Grid Ref: SK 364875 (Landranger 111, Pathfinder 743)

Discovering Industrial Sheffield

On a man-made island created in the twelfth century when water was diverted from the River Don along a a goit to drive the manorial corn mill, and reputedly named after armourer Kelham Homer who had a grinding workshop here in 1637, is Kelham Island Industrial Museum.

It occupies premises formerly used as a power station which, from 1899, supplied electricity to Sheffield's new trams. The museum celebrates the life and work of industrial Sheffield and houses the mighty River Don Engine, at 12,000 horsepower the most powerful working steam engine in Europe. The skill of the self-employed 'Little Mesters' always attracts interest, whilst in the Melting Shop children can clock on to enjoy the experience of life as a piece of steel, including being rolled and hammered! The great Bessemer Converter (one of a pair) at the museum entrance came from British Steel's Workington works, its last 'blow' in 1974 marking the end of the process in Britain. Kelham and its environs is a great place to gain a sense of Sheffield's relatively recent past and therefore better understand today's rapidly changing city.

Site: Alma Street, Sheffield. (Parking available.) The museum opens Mon–Thurs 10am–4pm, Sun 11am–4.45.pm, closed Fri & Sat.

Grid Ref: SK 352883 (Landranger 110 or 111, Pathfinder 743)

The Last Conical Furnace

By 1843, Sheffield was producing ninety per cent of British steel and almost half of all European output. Converting or cementation furnaces (using iron bars), easily recognised from the outside by their conical, bottle-like chimneys, were in such demand that over 200 were built in the Sheffield area. The last surviving example, built in 1848 and now restored, was one of five in steelworks that Daniel Doncaster began in his father's orchard seventeen years earlier. The top section was damaged in a 1940 air raid, so it was rebuilt with an anti-glare blackout device. It had a capacity of about 35 tons and was last operated between October 1951 and January 1952.

Site: Midland Bank car park, Doncaster Street, Sheffield.

Grid Ref: SK 348880 (Landranger 110 or 111, Pathfinder 743)

Green Lane Works

Anyone with an interest in industrial architecture could not fail to be impressed by the gatehouse at the headquarters of engineering firm W A Tyzack. Described as a 'Tripartite triumphal arch' by Pevsner, it was built in 1860 for Henry Hoole in celebration of his mayoral year. Hoole & Robson's foundry collaborated with the distinguished designer Alfred Stevens, and exhibited choice products at the Great Exhibition of 1851: an ornate fender, described in the illustrated catalogue as 'remarkable for the grace of the design', and a fire-grate 'richly decorated and admirably constructed'.

Returning to the gateway, the key-stone of the archway is in the form of a female head, and there are relief panels of Vulcan and Art over the pedestrian entrances on either side. The entire edifice (restored by Tyzacks) is surmounted by an elegant cupola and clock, and under the classical pediment the legend GREEN LANE WORKS can be seen in striking gold relief.

Site: Green Lane, Sheffield.

Grid Ref: SK 350882 (Landranger 110 or 111, Pathfinder 743)

A Showpiece of Industrial Architecture

Supertram now glides passed the front and skiers whiz down the slopes of the hillside behind the Globe Works. Its classical façade could easily be mistaken for a school or public building.

These early works were built in 1825 for Ibbotson & Roebuck, steel refiners, and manufacturers of scythes, saws, fenders and knives. Ibbotson was not the most popular of employers since we know he was attacked by 'ratteners' or saboteurs in 1843; and was even cited in Frederich Engels' *Condition of the Working Class in England* (1844). Cutlery and edge-tool firm John Walters & Co (later Unwin & Rodgers) succeeded Ibbotson in 1865, but many small concerns were also associated with the building, including Sheffield's last hand-cutters of files and rasps (until 1980). The future of this showpiece example of industrial architecture was in doubt after a serious fire in 1978, but it was rescued and given a new lease of life via a £1.5 million restoration in 1988-90.

A remnant of another of Ibbotson's enterprises, converted from the former Sheffield workhouse, can be seen in Alma Street, close to Kelham Island Museum, and now owned by Richardsons, the modern Laser knife manufacturer.

Site: Penistone Road, Sheffield.

Grid Ref: SK 348883 (Landranger 110 or 111, Pathfinder 743)

Hill Top Chapel

At Attercliffe, lying back from the busy road, is a small chapel-of-ease of the parish of Sheffield, built in 1629, largely with the patronage of the Bright and Spencer families. The initials of two stonemasons, Thomas Arnalde and Henry Barber, are still extant over the north doorway.

The original structure was much larger than the building of today, which was reduced to its present dimensions in 1897 after suffering many years of neglect. Restored and re-dedicated in 1909, its small cemetery contains many worthies of the locality, notably the Swallows of New Hall, Staniforths of Darnall, the Machins and Sorbys, but its most famous monument is to Benjamin Huntsman *(see page 16)*, inventor of the crucible steel process.

Site: Hill Top Cemetery, Attercliffe Common, off Attercliffe Road (A6178).
Grid Ref: SK 383895 (Landranger 110 or 111, Pathfinder 743)

'The Mynster of the Moores'

After the antiquary Roger Dodsworth visited Ecclesfield in 1620 he wrote: 'The church is called (and that deservedly) by the vulger the Mynster of the Moores, being the fairest church for stone, wood, glase, and neat keeping, that ever I came in ...'.

Behind the church, in the vicarage, lived a literary family — the Gattys. Dr Alfred Gatty, sixty-three years as vicar, wrote on Sheffield history and left us a description of the parish in *A Life at One Living* (1884). His wife Margaret, and their daughter, Juliana Ewing, were very popular Victorian writers of children's stories. Margaret also wrote on seaweeds and zoophytes, and sundials; and in true scientific spirit allowed herself to be chloroformed as an example for the parish. Gatty's curate, Jonathan Eastwood, published a parish history in 1862. Reverend Joseph Hunter (1783-1861), the great historian of Sheffield and South Yorkshire who spent most of his life in Bath and London (where he became an assistant keeper of the Public Records in the new Public Record Office), chose to be buried at Ecclesfield. The research tradition has been kept alive in recent times with, for example, *The Village of Ecclesfield* (1968), the first of Professor David Hey's excellent books on local and family history.

Site: Church Street (B6087), Ecclesfield.

Grid Ref: SK 353942 (Landranger 110, Pathfinder 726)

Huntsman's Memorial

The family tombstone and a simple modern plaque of Benjamin Huntsman, inventor of the crucible steelmaking process, can be seen in Hill Top Cemetery at Attercliffe.

Huntsman came from a Quaker family at Epworth, where he was an apprentice clockmaker. After setting up in business in Doncaster, he may have become frustrated by the inconsistent quality of imported steel used for watch springs and pendulums, and began experiments by re-melting blister steel in small crucibles. He moved to a cottage in Handsworth in 1742, continued to work in secrecy, but by 1751 his innovative process had such commercial promise that new works were established on the east side of Leeds Road, Attercliffe (and from c1770 on Worksop Road), latterly living in a house now known as the Britannia Inn. He died on the 20th June 1776, aged seventy-two. Like Thomas Boulsover, he can be regarded as a great pioneer of the Sheffield steel industry, and so of international importance.

Site : Hill Top Chapel Cemetery, Attercliffe Common, Sheffield.
Grid Ref: SK 382894 (Landranger 110 or 111, Pathfinder 743)

Meadowhall

Domes have become a distinctive architectural feature of the modern large-scale leisure centres of South Yorkshire, as can be seen at Barnsley (Metrodome) and Doncaster (the Dome), but Sheffield's outstanding example can be seen at Meadowhall, in the Lower Don Valley, where construction began in June 1988 on a site formerly occupied by Hadfield Steel Works.

Twenty-seven months and £270 million later, Meadowhall Shopping and

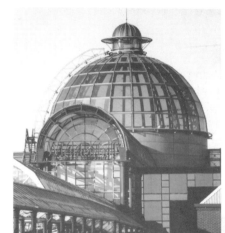

Leisure Centre opened to the public on the 4th September 1990 — a remarkable achievement given the huge scale of the project. With over 270 shops, 12,000 free parking spaces, its own rail and bus stations and, from 1994, the Supertram link, Meadowhall has been a huge commercial success. The centre was designed on two levels with seven 'anchor' stores: Savacentre, Marks & Spencer, Debenhams, House of Fraser, C & A, Boots and W H Smith; and there are six themed areas: Market Street (convenience stores), High Street (main retail section), the Arcade (fashion) and Park Lane (a mixture of quality retailers), Coca-Cola Oasis (a spectacular 'Mediterranean' showpiece central court with giant Vidiwall screen, 1,400 seats, twenty eating places and Warner Bros multiplex cinema) and the Lanes (speciality and cosmopolitan shops).

Site: adjacent to Junction 34 of the M1, north-east of Sheffield.

Grid Ref: SK 395923 (Landranger 110 or 111)

Teemers

This magnificent celebration of crucible steelmaking deserves more than a glance from Meadowhall shoppers. The commission is the work of Canadian sculpture Robin Bell whose studios are in Tuscany. The composition is based on a c1940s photograph taken at Kayser Ellisons.

'Teeming' was a four-man process, but Robin omitted a nine-year old boy for reasons of political correctness since it may have 'promoted' child labour, or even under-age drinking. Workers lost so much sweat that body fluids needed frequent replacement in the form of an 'ale allowance' of four pints (7 litres) per shift, and the youngest 'got the ale in'. The teemer on the right had to lift an enormous weight — around thirteen stones (73kg) — and when the molten metal was poured, temperatures were so high that faces could blister. The damp cloth in his mouth provided some protection from fumes and combated dryness, but many workers died whilst still young men. The fifteen year old apprentice is skimming slag off the steel. The 8' 3" (2.5m) tall figure on the left is holding a 'dozzle' which captured impurities. Robin put his own face on the teemer, and the face of the nephew of former Italian heavyweight boxer Primo Carnera on the dozzler.

Site: Meadowhall Shopping and Leisure Centre, off junction 34 of the M1.

Grid Ref: SK 395923 (Landranger 110 or 111)

A Bright Home

It is remarkable that Carbrook Hall has survived to the present day in an area that has witnessed so much industrial, commercial and modern development.

Carbrook was the seventeenth century home of the Brights, one of Sheffield's most prominent families We know that Thomas Bright was in possession of the house in 1623, and the next owner was Stephen Bright, who was Lord of the Manor of Ecclesall in 1638. John Bright, who inherited the estate, was a staunch Parliamentarian during the Civil War. With the help of Gell's Derbyshire troops, he took Sheffield Castle without a fight, but the 'victory' was short-lived — the castle succumbed to Royalist forces, supported by townspeople, two years later. The restored exterior of Carbrook has four-light mullioned and transomed windows on the gable facing the main road, but the main attraction is the interior, which has an exceptionally fine room with a fireplace and plaster ceiling built for Stephen Bright — and fine panelling.

Site: Carbrook, opposite Meadowhall Retail Park, off the A 6178.

Grid Ref: SK 386898 (Landranger 110 or 111, Pathfinder 743/726)

Hollin Busk Mine

Probably one of the most underrated social aspects of rapidly developing industrialisation in nineteenth century South Yorkshire was the human consequences of the huge demand for refractory materials for use in the manufacturing of steel. Where geological conditions were favourable — such as at the western edge of the coal measures around Deepcar — fireclay and ganister, used for lining furnaces, was mined, but in conditions often worse than in most collieries of the period. Here miners suffered badly from the inhalation of dust in the process of of their work, many of them dying young.

In the absence of statistics, the family histories of local people provide us with the our most meaningful appreciation of working conditions. Job Elliott, my great-grandfather, aged forty-seven, and his eldest son George, thirty, both died as a result of working in the Deepcar mines. The headgear, small winding-wheel and spoil mound of Hollin Busk Colliery and Clay Mine is a lone and near-forgotten survivor of such hard and sad times.

Site: the junction of Hollin Busk Lane and Cockshot Lane, Deepcar.

Grid Ref: SK 277973 (Landranger 110, Pathfinder 726)

An Ancient Pennine Village

Bolsterstone is an ancient Pennine village, but most of its houses are clustered around a relatively modern church. The settlement has associations with a pre-Christian past, whilst Walders Low, a nearby burial mound on a hilltop over 1,000 feet (300m) above sea level, is a reminder of Saxon occupation.

With its 'castle', Bolsterstone-in-Waldershelf was a medieval manor of some importance, with a chapel extant from at least 1412. Around 1650 Christopher Dickinson, deposed vicar of Penistone, came here and was described by the Puritan diarist Adam Eyre as 'a man of scandalous life and conversation and a frequenter of alehouses'. Later, in 1685, Reverend Marsh of Bolsterstone was dispatched to York gaol for allowing clandestine marriages. Granted a reprieve by the archbishop, he returned as vicar in 1696. The old church was pulled down by Reverend Bland in 1791, replaced by a building said to be so ugly that Gatty of Ecclesfield (see page 15) described it as 'more like a factory'. The present church was built between 1872 and 1879 during the incumbency of Rev Reginald Wilson and cost £7,200.

The Bolsterstone Male Voice Choir was formed in 1934 by a few members of the church choir. Today it is recognised as one of Britain's best choirs, has won many prestigious prizes and is developing an international reputation.

Site: ten miles (16km) north-west of Sheffield, off the A616.

Grid Ref: SK 271968 (Landranger 110, Pathfinder 726)

Resurrectionists Watch Out!

The gruesome practice of body-snatching was of sufficient concern to the citizens (my paternal ancestors included) of Bradfield — whose large churchyard was sited near the top of a prominent hill — that a purpose-built watch tower was built overlooking the entrance.

Known with appropriate black humour as 'resurrectionists', there were in fact a number of local characters whose dark deeds were the result of rewards offered by tutor

surgeons such as the notorious Professor Knox of Edinburgh, who offered £10 per corpse for use in his anatomy 'master classes'. Irish opportunists Burke and Hare made things a little easier for themselves (before being caught out) by advancing the process of mortality, murdering a few unsuspecting persons and shipping them off 'when still warm'. Country churchyards, especially those in remote settings, were particularly susceptible to the 'corpse trade'. Understandably, as well as practical anti-theft measures such as the building of watch houses, there was great public indignigation prior to the passing of the Anatomy Act of 1829 which effectively put an end to this most heinous of crimes.

Site: St Nicholas Church, High Bradfield.

Grid Ref: SK 268925 (Landranger 110, Pathfinder 726)

The Round House that isn't

A small but distinctive group of buildings occupy a lonely spot where three roads meet at the edge of Hallam Moors, five miles (8km) south-west of Sheffield.

Generally known as the Round House, though it is in fact purposefully octagonal (allowing the occupant a good view of the three roads), Ringinglow tollhouse was erected in 1795 as the Barber Fields Cupola Tollhouse (a lead-smelting furnace was located nearby, at Bole Hill) sited where the 1758 turnpike road from Sheffield diverged

to Fox House and Chapel-en-le Frith. Its location paid off in the early years — a substantial £421 was collected in 1797 — but was redundant from about 1812 when the present A625 Banner Cross to Fox House road was made, and new toll cottages established. Traffic also declined on the Chapel road due to the opening of the Snake Pass route in 1821, significantly the year in which the tollhouse was converted into a private dwelling. The adjacent Norfolk Arms (formerly the Ringinglow Inn) was also established here to take advantage of new turnpike traffic.

Site: Ringinglow, five miles (8km) south-west of Sheffield.

Grid Ref: SK 291838 (Landranger 110, Pathfinder 743)

Past Forward at Abbeydale

Sheffield's greatest asset was its skilled craftspeople. It is a tribute to the city council, museum service and many enthusiasts that — as we approach the millennium — vestiges of past skill has been kept alive through both the permanent and occasional working days when the public can see at first-hand the work of scythe grinder Ron Staley at the Abbeydale Industrial Hamlet and the 'Little Mesters' at Kelham Island Museum *(see page 10)*.

The eighteenth century water-powered site at Abbeydale, with its four waterwheels, associated machinery and unique crucible steel furnace, has come a long way since the writer brought school parties to the site in the early 1970s. The historic complex of buildings is the first industrial site to be given a grade I listing by English Heritage and has become a major tourist attraction, a status which will hopefully assist in further funding.

Site: Abbeydale Road South, Sheffield 7. Unfortunately the museum is now 'mothballed', but there is public access to see the 'Little Mesters'.
Grid Ref: SK 326820 (Landranger 111, Pathfinder 743)

The House of a Yeoman Farmer

In the Tudor period, most town houses in Sheffield were timber-framed, and this was also the traditional method of building for farmhouses and barns in the surrounding countryside.

Bishops' House, built in about 1500, is a fine example of a prosperous yeoman farmer's or minor gentleman's house. Its east wing contains the hall — originally open to the rafters — along with a kitchen and chamber (a floor was inserted in the early seventeenth century). Further rooms were provided when a cross-wing was added in about 1550. Prior to around 1850, when the building was known as 'Old Hall', barns and outbuildings were also to be seen.

The local family long associated with the house were the Blythes. Nicholas Blythe, who died in 1631, successfully combined farming with scythe-making, and was able to afford improvements such as new fireplaces, panelling and decorative plasterwork, whilst his son, also called William, built a stone extension, possibly using materials from Sheffield Castle. After extensive restoration the house was opened as a museum in 1976, and offers the public a unique opportunity to view a late medieval dwelling at close quarters.

Site: Meersbook Park, Norton Lees, about two miles (3km) south of Sheffield. The museum is open Wed–Sat 10am–4.30pm, Sun 11am–4.30pm.

Grid Ref: SK 354840 (Landranger 111, Pathfinder 743)

'Chantryland'

Sir Francis Legatt Chantry (1781-1841) chose the small but pleasant country churchyard of St James's, Norton, as his final resting place, despite his fame as one of the nation's greatest sculptors and therefore worthy of commemoration in Westminster Abbey.

His wish was a most appropriate recognition of his childhood and early life. The son of a carpenter, when Chantry was a boy he delivered milk, carried on a donkey, from Norton to Sheffield, and worked for a grocer. After serving his apprenticeship to a woodcarver and shopkeeper, he set himself up as a portrait painter in Paradise Square, charging two to three guineas in 1802. He moved to London, continuing with portraits and carvings, but increasingly gaining a reputation as a talented sculptor. His commissions included statues of George III, James Watt, Sir Walter Scott and the naturalist Sir Joseph Banks.

Thirteen years after his death, a granite obelisk — paid for by public subscription and designed by his friend Philip Hardwick RA — was erected on the once-spacious green at Norton, inscribed with just one word: CHANTRY.

Site: St James's Church and village green, Norton.

Grid Ref: SK 359822 (Landranger 110, Pathfinder 743)

Viewing the Chase

Very little remains of the once-extensive Manor Lodge, situated in the medieval deer park high above Sheffield, the splendid residence of the earls of Shrewsbury, but at the edge of its grounds is the 'Turret House', a restored Elizabethan building of three storeys, the gatehouse of the lodge.

When Mary Queen of Scots was placed in the custody of George Talbot, the sixth earl, he was obliged, at great expense, to enlarge the manor to provide appropriate accommodation for the queen and her household. It is unlikely that the Turret House was built for this purpose, as it lacked both the proportions or stately facilities. However, Mary may well have been invited to use the roof of the building for another fashionable purpose — to view the chase. Tudor parks often had hunting towers where guests could also take shelter and receive refreshments. Here the earl could entertain in a delightful top floor room which had a fine plaster ceiling and his family coat of arms displayed over the fireplace.

Site: Manor Lane, off City Road, Sheffield.

Grid Ref: SK 375864 (Landranger 110 or 111, Pathfinder 743)

Shepherd Wheel

Abbeydale Industrial Hamlet deserves accolade, but a more realistic impression of working conditions can be had by visiting Shepherd Wheel — despite its picturesque location.

J E White's *Report upon the metal manufactures of the Sheffield district*, presented as evidence to the Government's Children's Employment Commission of 1865, included Shepherd Wheel as a typical example of the kind of unhealthy and unsafe working conditions in small water-powered workshops along Sheffield's rivers. Two employees, Benjamin Wildgoose (aged forty-four) and Samuel Hind (fifty-four), had worked there since they were nine and ten years old, and described the cold, damp conditions, dark evenings working by candlelight, dangerous machinery and the occasional bursting of a grindstone. The property was rented by a Mr Shepherd in 1794 who employed a team of ten grinders, probably processing a variety of knives for both domestic and specialist use. The 'Potar Wheele' mentioned in the 1584 will of Benjamin Beighton could well be the same site as the premises later occupied by Shepherd. With its overshot waterwheel, dam and historic premises, Shepherd Wheel will continue to attract visitors, providing the hard task of maintenance and restoration is supported.

Site: Whitely Woods. Main access via Hangingwater Road, via A625 (Ecclesall Road), Sheffield.Open Wed, Fri, Sat 10am–5pm, Sun 11am–5pm, closes 4.30pm in winter.

Grid Ref: SK 318854 (Landranger 110 or 111, Pathfinder 743)

Two Contrasting Monuments

A stone sculpture of a First World War soldier serves as a poignant and yet all-too-familiar reminder of an event that impacted on every South Yorkshire village. Across the lane can be found a modern commemoration of a more ancient military event. A sandstone monolith incorporates a shield-shaped plaque inscribed with a dragon and the words:

KING ECGBERT OF WESSEX LED HIS ARMY TO DORE IN THE YEAR AD 829 AGAINST KING EANRED OF NORTHUMBRIA BY WHOSE SUBMISSION KING ECGBERT BECAME FIRST OVERLORD OF ALL ENGLAND

Dore lay on the ancient and important border that divided Northumbria from Wessex. We also know from the *Anglo-Saxon Chronicle* that Dore's strategic and political importance was further confirmed in AD 942 when Edmund, son of Edward the Elder, conquered the Danes of Mercia 'as far as where Dore divides'. The counties of Yorkshire and Derbyshire, and the diocese of York and Litchfield, also separated at Dore.

Site: Dore village green/Vicarage Lane.

Grid Ref: SK 309811 (Landranger 110, Pathfinder 743)

Round and About Rotherham

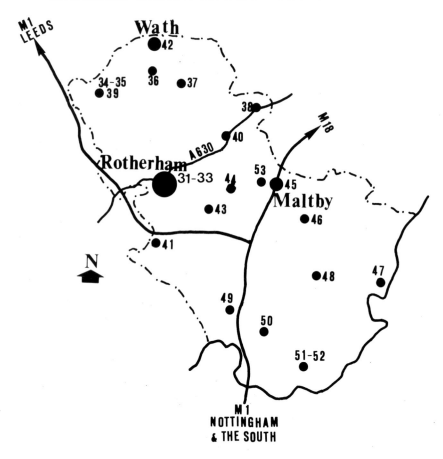

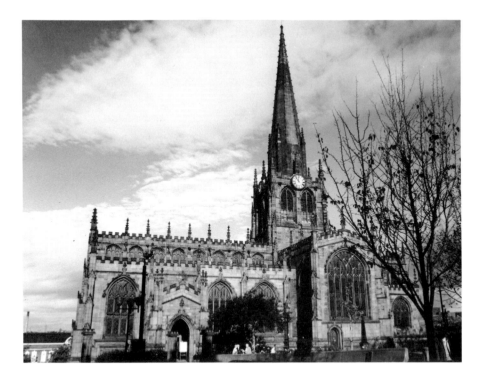

Saints and Sinners

All Saints', Rotherham, is the most impressive medieval town church in South Yorkshire. Of cruciform layout, on an ancient site, it dates mostly from the fifteenth century, built largely by the monks of Rufford Abbey. The most spectacular exterior feature is the tower and spire, which soars 180 feet (55m) above its fan-vaulted crossing.

Work began in 1409, financed by the sale of indulgences to repentent sinners who were promised relief from purgatory. Eighteenth century and Victorian restoration, the latter by Sir George Gilbert Scott, has not detracted from the overwhelmingly Perpendicular grandeur. The south chancel chapel is generally attributed to one of the most famous sons of the town, Thomas Rotherham, Bishop of Lincoln (but soon elected archbishop of York), for use by the priests at his nearby red-brick College of Jesus which he had founded in 1482-3. The nave has a fine panelled ceiling, there are original choir stalls in the chancel, late medieval bench ends and a Jacobean pulpit. Local mason-architect John Platt was responsible for one of the monuments, to Mrs Buck, completed in 1752. Another commemorates the Masborough boat launching accident of 1841 when fifty young men drowned.

Site: All Saints' Square, central Rotherham.

Grid Ref: SK 428929 (Landranger 111, Pathfinder 727)

A Rare Bridge Chapel

Chapels built on or by bridges were a fairly common feature in the Middle Ages. Today only a handful survive, two of them in the old West Riding, at Wakefield and this one at Rotherham. Travellers were able to say prayers of thanks for their safe arrival and expected to make an offering, in effect a toll.

The Rotherham example can be dated by the 1483 will of local grammar school master John Bokying, who bequeathed three shillings and four pence 'to the fabric of the chapel to be built on Rotherham Bridge'. It was constructed in a fashionable style to match the parish church. After the dissolution of chantries in 1547, the chapel came under the care of the Feoffees. There was a brief return to religious service in the 1550s, followed by many years of neglect until, in 1681-2, the chapel was repaired and used as an almshouse. From 1779 until about 1826 it was used as jail and after 1888 as a residence. The chapel was restored and re-consecrated in 1924, having previously been used as a tobacconist's shop. Dedicated to Our Lady, the chapel is still used for services.

Site: Rotherham Bridge, immediately to the west of the town centre.

Grid Ref: SK 426930 (Landranger 111, Pathfinder 727)

Clifton House and Park

Clifton House was built in 1782-3 to the design of John Carr of York. It was commissioned by Joshua Walker (1750-1815) the well-known Rotherham iron-founder. Carr's original two-storey design produced an attractive façade of five bays, including a central three-bay pediment which encompasses a Palladian window and a classic entrance porch or portico. The interior contains a fine staircase and hall floors in Derbyshire marble by the Rotherham mason-architect John Platt. The Owen family succeeded the Walkers in 1860. The surrounding garden and estate were purchased for £25,000 by the corporation in 1891 and opened as a public park. Two years later the house opened as a museum for the inhabitants of the town and district. An extension was opened in 1974.

Site: Clifton Lane (A6021), about half a mile (0.8km) from the town centre.
The museum is open Mon–Thurs & Sat 10am–5pm, Sun 2.30–5pm, closes 4.30pm in winter.
Grid Ref: SK 435928 (Landranger 111, Pathfinder 727)

The Enlightened Earl

By the early nineteenth century, Wentworth, with its great house and park, enhanced by a series of striking follies and a myriad of conversational garden features, all newly integrated into the landscape by Humphrey Repton, was a small but thriving village. But further building was required to meet the changing needs of the Fitzwilliam family, their estate and the community. New cottages and estate buildings, a new school and eventually a magnificent new church was constructed, giving the village the distinctive appearance that visitors recognise today.

But perhaps the most underrated innovation was the provision of a mechanics institute, built on Main Street in 1835, eighteen years before the institute in Rotherham

opened. A mechanics institute had been established in Sheffield just three years before Wentworth, sponsors assuring local businessmen that the increase in knowledge would not cause a 'want of respect to their superiors, or disobey their masters'. The earl's motives are likely to have been more enlightened, appreciating the intrinsic and moral value of education for his workers and their families, though aristocratic influence is plain to see in its battlemented façade, from the prominently-placed armoral shield down to 'estate green' painted railings.

Site: Main Street (B 6090), Wentworth.

Grid Ref: SK 387982 (Landranger 111, Pathfinder 726)

Through a Needle's Eye

Of the Wentworth follies, the Needle's Eye is the smallest but probably the most graceful, and certainly the most intriguing. It consists of an ogee archway which spanned an old coach road that once ran from Wentworth towards Brampton Bierlow. It is said, by Pevsner, to date from 1780, but research by Arthur Clayton has shown that Lord Malton, who became the first marquis of Rockingham in 1746, referred to an obelisk in Lee Wood in his 1722-3 building expenses, and again in 1743. This may well have been the Needle's Eye. In 1768 Arthur Young could have been referring to the Needle's Eye when he wrote 'at no distance from the pyramid [Hoober Stand] is the arch, another building which was raised as an object to decorate the view from the Ionic Temple'.

Of the stories associated with the arch, its use as a 'testing ground' for driving horses and carriages is the most common. The theory was apparently put to the test by Earl Fitzwilliam at the time of the First World War — by driving a gun carriage through! However, the idea of his aristocratic forbears driving a coach and pair at speed through such a narrow space — and after a night's revelling — was almost certainly a myth. The monument's purpose was aesthetic rather than athletic: designed and sited to please the noble eye.

Site: Lee Wood, by footpath from Coley Lane (opposite junction with Street Lane).

Grid Ref: SK 397988 (Landranger 111, Pathfinder 726)

A World-Famous Pottery

The early nineteenth century Waterloo or Rockingham Kiln at Swinton is virtually all that remains of a world-renowned pottery. Joseph Flint established his works here in 1741, but it was under the ownership of the Brameld family — with support from Earl Fitzwilliam — that the pottery gained an international reputation. Bankruptcy was avoided in 1815 only after further financial help from the earl, whose patronage was recognised by Brameld's adoption of the name Rockingham and the use of the griffin trademark. Meeting an order from William III for a 200 piece service was achieved but at great cost, the works closing down in 1842.

The distinctive kiln saw subsequent service as an isolation hospital and, as recently as 1951, as a dwelling. It is now in the care of Rotherham Council. 'Rockingham' is much sought after by porcelain enthusiasts all over the world, but it is appropriate that the best collection can be seen in the town's Clifton Museum *(see page 33)*.

Site: Swinton is about four miles (6.5km) north of Rotherham; the kiln can be reached on foot from Blackamoor Road (B 6092) where there is a small car park.

Grid Ref: SK 440988 (Landranger 111, Pathfinder 727)

Waddington's Boatyard

Anyone interested in South Yorkshire canals are likely to have some knowledge of 'Waddingtons' of Swinton. This well known family business, originally in boat-building and repairing which branched out in the 1920s into carrying, was established by Ernest Waddington and his brother, and continued by Ernest's son Victor who became manager of the firm in 1923.

When fleets of barges ceased operating in the 1950s and 1960s, Waddingtons purchased many 'redundant' vessels, soon becoming the main carriers on the Sheffield and South Yorkshire Navigation. Victor Waddington has many achievements in the promotion and improvement of inland waterways, especially during the 1980s. The rebuilt Swinton Lock was renamed Waddington Lock in honour of his 'long and enthusiastic association with the Navigation and neighbouring waterways'.

Site: the boatyard lies at the junction of the Sheffield and South Yorkshire Navigation and the now-derelict Dearne and Dove Canal at Swinton, close to the aptly named Ship public house.

Grid Ref: SK 465991 (Landranger 111, Pathfinder 727)

A Horse Engine-house

Many arable farms had 'engine-houses' powered by horses, and where they survive (rarely with machinery intact) they are interesting architectural features.

Most date from the late eighteenth and early nineteenth centuries. They were usually attached to one long wall of the barn, though some were free-standing, varying in form from circular or semi-circular to polygonal or square/rectangular. Their purpose was to provide power — via fixed poles and a crown wheel attached to a vertical axle — to drive the new threshing machines that many farms were beginning to use. The abandonment of traditional hand-flails did not go down well with agricultural labourers, who felt threatened by mechanisation. Horses, usually four at a time, trod a path between 24 and 26 feet (7.3 to 7.9 m) in diameter. A day's threshing might require two horse teams.

It is pleasing when such attractive yet functional buildings have been restored, even when converted to other uses. The technique for using horses for mechanical purposes was by no means new to the area, as the winding 'whim' or 'gin' had been in use at pit heads since the Middle Ages.

Site: this converted example, now called Holly Bank Fold, can be seen on the east side of the A630 (Doncaster–Sheffield road) at Hooton Roberts, across from the Earl of Strafford pub/restaurant.

Grid Ref: SK 485971 (Landranger 111, Pathfinder 727)

A Plague Stone?

About a mile (1.5km) away from Wentworth village is a curious short stone shaft, almost hidden from view, which is believed to have had associations with the Plague, endemic in Britain from about 1350 to its sudden disappearance after 1666.

Central and local government tried to eradicate the disease by a variety of measures. New research suggests that to escape the full impact was probably as much due to good luck as good management. Wayside stones were supposedly placed at the edge of villages, their upper part hollowed out to contain diluted vinegar. Into this liquor, infected villagers placed coins, to be picked out by outsiders in return for food which would be left at the stone. Such stones and such 'stories' are difficult to authenticate, but the Wentworth example clearly has a carved and bevelled edge basin, and we do know that plague was present in the locality. The Wath parish register records an outbreak starting at Swinton on the 27th June 1646, ending on the 5th October of the same year, accounting for fifty-nine deaths.

Site: Coley Lane (off Cortworth Lane, B 6090), opposite Street Lane (and hamlet of the same name), just to the right of a gate for the footpath leading to Lee Wood and the Needle's Eye monument.

Grid Ref: SK 398987 (Landranger 111, Pathfinder 726)

A Saxon Cross?

The lower part of an ancient cross can be seen in St Leonard's churchyard at Thrybergh, one of two local examples. It was placed there — for safe-keeping — several years ago, from a more vulnerable site near the village. Medieval crosses are difficult to date, the deeply incised design on this example having both pre-Conquest and later medieval features. Could it be a Saxon piece re-carved later? It is certainly one of the earliest and most interesting surviving crosses in the county. The truncated shaft is 4' 4" (1.3m) high and in section measures 14" by 10" (35cm x 25cm). It is composed of yellow limestone (in contrast to the Coal Measure sandstone of the church), probably carried from the nearby Magnesian Limestone belt a couple of miles (3km) away. The west face is shown in the photograph. The lowest part consist of a figure reading a book, set within a pointed arch. Above it is a leaf motif and some kind of animal arranged beneath the feet of another human figure. We can also see the north face, which has a ring-twist pattern with pellets and acanthus.

Site: the south-east corner of St Leonard's churchyard, Thrybergh.

Grid Ref: SK 467955 (Landranger 111, Pathfinder 727)

The Glass Cone

South Yorkshire has a long tradition of glassmaking. The first works was established in 1632 at Wentworth on ground leased from the earl of Strafford, but only slightly outlasted the earl's execution in 1641. More successful sites developed from about 1650 at Silkstone near Barnsley, and in Bolsterstone parish (Stocksbridge).

William Fenny, who managed the Bolsterstone works in the early eighteenth century, fell out with Mary Blackburn, his mother-in-law and widow of the owner. Mary, in her will, barred Fenny from making glass within ten miles (16km), so he moved to Catcliffe where he founded a new works in 1740, producing bottles, flint and window glass. Two cone furnaces were built, the shell of the brick one still surviving and now a distinctive and protected monument. Fenny's finances were exhausted by capital costs: building the surviving cone would have required some 120,000 bricks. By 1759 the Catcliffe works was taken over by the May family, and from 1833 by a partnership, Blunn & Booth. It closed in 1884, though had a brief awakening in 1901. Threatened with demolition in the 1960s, it has now been restored, one of only five in the British Isles.

Site: it stands within a sheltered housing complex, with access via the west side of Main Street, Catcliffe.

Grid Ref: SK 425997 (Landranger 111, Pathfinder 744)

Sobering Cells

Built in the early nineteenth century, the lock-up at Wath-upon-Dearne (shown here before recent conversion) is a rare survival of the days when law and order was the responsibility of the village constable. Constables were elected annually, usually one per township and had considerable administrative duties, even though some could hardly read or write.

The ground floor contained two cells, each with a stone toilet. The upper room, with its fireplace, was for the convenience of the constable or his guard. The lock-up would have been used for the short-term custody of minor offenders such as drunkards and vagrants, or as a holding place prior to transportation to, for example, the House of Correction at Wakefield. The listed building has been converted into a private one-bedroomed residence. The cells have been turned into a kitchen and bathroom, whilst the constable's quarter has been changed into a living room, its fireplace retained and a sleeping gallery created in the roof space. Almost hidden by modern housing, the historic lock-up is no longer in danger or dereliction and demolition.

Site: four miles (6.5km) north of Rotherham, on the east side of Well Lane, about fifty yards (45m) west of All Saints Church; best seen via Thornhill Place, off Church Street.
Grid Ref: SE 434008 (Landranger 111, Pathfinder 716)

A Magnificent Medieval Barn

Whiston is rightly proud of its magnificent timber-framed long barn of nine bays. It has been identified by archaeologists using dendrochronological (tree-ring) dating as probably the oldest secular building in the region. Along with a similar example at Gunthwaite, near Penistone, South Yorkshire has two exceptional aisled-hall barns.

The original structure appears to have been constructed in the thirteenth century, probably by the Furnival family, and later extended and the roof refashioned. Stone cladding was probably the last major phase of building. By about 1980 the fabric of the barn was in a very poor condition and the entire building at risk of complete dereliction. Fortunately, restoration work towards the end of the decade, including the provision of a new thatched roof, has not only ensured its survival as a national monument but also provided an excellent community resource. It is used by a variety of local groups and hosts popular special events such as antique fairs. On display in the barn is an interesting series of recently-completed heritage tapestries.

Site: Whiston village is about three miles (5km) south-east of Rotherham. The barn is best seen from Chaff Lane and Chaff Close via High Street.

Grid Ref: SK 447900 (Landranger 111, Pathfinder 727)

World-famous Grindstones Made Here

In the nineteenth century Wickersley was a small but thriving agricultural and quarrying community, and had developed a worldwide reputation for the making of grindstones, used in the cutlery and associated tool trades.

Understandably, its early manufacturing associations were linked to Sheffield where grinding the edge of steel tools was a vital requisite of quality products. From the seventeenth century it was found that stone from Wickersley quarries was of ideal consistency for this purpose. Baines's West Riding directory of 1822 informed readers that 'upwards of 5,000 of these stones of various sizes, from one to six feet [0.3-2m] in diameter, are annually made here, and sent by land carriage to the Sheffield manufactures'. Forty-two years later twenty-two quarry owners were listed in White's directory, and extant records from the Roddis quarry shows that stones were ordered from Argentina, Australia, Belgium, Denmark, Egypt, Holland, Norway, Palestine, Sweden and America in the 1850s. The men employed to extract, hew, shape, cut and cart the stone worked long and hard at their task in difficult conditions.

Site: one of two grindstones is mounted over the village sign on the A631 (Bawtry) road.
Grid Ref: SK 485920 (Landranger 111, Pathfinder 727)

Good Ale for Nothing

A most curious inscription appears on a lozenge-shaped plaque on the face of the Cottages guesthouse at Maltby. Under the personal initials 'WTS' is the legend COME TOMORROW AND YOU SHALL HAVE GOOD ALE FOR NOTHING DO NOT FORGET and the year '1686'.

The style, arrangement of letters and phraseology is in keeping with other seventeenth century motifs on, for example, pottery and church monuments, though the raised (as against 'cut') lettering is somewhat unusual. Situated close to the 'highway' from Sheffield and Rotherham leading towards Bawtry and Blyth, it is likely to have associations with an inn or alehouse. A survey of guest beds and stabling 'throughout the land' in 1686 shows a considerable growth of facilities since Tudor times, linked of course to the growth of trade. But in the locality, most inns were small. Rotherham had just 66 guest beds and stabling for only 72 horses according to the 1686 returns. This in contrast to a fashionable centre such as Doncaster, which could accommodate 206 guests and 453 horses. However, the small village of Wombwell, because of its use as a stopping place on the London–Halifax road, had 24 guest beds, almost as many as the town of Huddersfield.

Site: the junction of High Street (A631) and Blyth Road (A634).

Grid Ref: SK 528921 (Landranger 111, Pathfinder 727)

'Bare ruin'd choirs where late the sweet birds sang'

Founded in 1147, Roche Abbey was one of eight Cistercian houses in the old county of Yorkshire. Part of the east end of the church are the only substantial remains, hardly surprising given the events following the dismissal of the monks in 1538. Michael Sherbrook, rector of Wickersley, described the plundering:

> *The church was the first thing that was put to spoil ... It would have pitied the Heart to see what tearing up of the Lead there was, and plucking up of Boards, and throwing down of the Sparres ... and all things of Price, either spoiled, carped away or defaced to the uppermost.*

What was left was eventually inherited by Thomas Lumley in 1723, but subsequently further remains were taken down and extensive areas covered on the advice of

England's most famous landscape gardener, Lancelot 'Capability' Brown. Today English Heritage are correct in hailing Roche's almost complete plan as exceptional, but credit should go to pioneering pre-First World War excavations, especially when Aldred, the tenth earl of Scarbrough, and his family were 'undoing' some of Brown's work. 'Spoiled' or not, visiting a deserted Roche on a cold winter's morning, with snow all around, one is aware of the silence, spirituality and tranquillity of this magnificent site.

Site: almost two miles (3km) south of Maltby, signposted off the A634 (Blyth) road.
Grid Ref: SK 544898 (Landranger 111, Pathfinder 744)

A Dovecote Saved from Ruin

In the medieval period the right of keeping pigeons was limited to a privileged few. By the end of the seventeenth century, restrictions were relaxed, and soon many farmhouses had some kind of dovecote or pigeon loft.

In the countryside of South Yorkshire many examples are still extant, though some are hidden from view, converted to other uses or simply not generally recognised. An exceptional showpiece example, dating from the eighteenth century, can be seen in the pleasant village of Letwell. Made of brick, with a magnesian limestone base and door surround, its octagonal shape and hipped roof supports a central bird-access cupola or lantern. Inside are hundreds of neatly-arranged nest-holes. A central revolving ladder or 'potence' was a convenient device for collecting eggs, squabs (young birds) and adult pigeons which were very useful sources of fresh food. Letwell villagers rallied to rescue the historic dovecote from possible ruin, raising funds for vital restoration work, and received an award from the Council for the Protection of Rural England for their efforts.

Site: Letwell is about five miles (8km) south-east of Maltby; access to the dovecote, which stands in the former cricket field known as the Croft, is via South Farm (Barker Hades Road).

Grid Ref: SK 563869 (Landranger 111, Pathfinder 744)

Education and Training for the Future: with a Sense of Community History

Many South Yorkshire rural communities have been transformed by the impact of coalmining, but Dinnington's case is exceptional. For centuries it remained a small settlement largely under the control of Athorps who were resident lords. As late as 1901 the population was only 258. Ten years later it had exploded to 4,897, and 6,438 people were recorded in the census of 1921. The reason for this metamorphosis was of course the sinking of Dinnington Colliery in 1902. Initially the pit sinkers were housed in make-do accommodation known as 'Tin Town' but soon model housing was built by the colliery company. In 1928 the Mining and Technical Institute was opened by Viscount Chelmsford, chair of the Miners' Welfare central committee. Built in red brick in a neo-classical style, its clock tower made it a distinctive landmark.

Mining courses ceased fifteen years ago, and in 1995 the pit and its outbuildings were obliterated from the landscape. Today the newly-expanded Rother Valley College, regarded as one of the most efficient and successful in the region, is the major employer in Dinnington, and a most appropriate location for the display of the miners' union banner.

Site: Dinnington is eight miles (13km) south-east of Rotherham. The college is situated on Doe Quarry Lane.

Grid Ref: SK 528866 (Landranger 111, Pathfinder 744)

Where Byron was 'a Slave to Impulse'

In 1772 the prolific York architect John Carr was commissioned by Lord Holderness to design a new mansion at Aston in the latest style. The result was a fairly conventional composition, though Carr's usual attention to symmetry remained: seven bays, with centre three projecting on both façades. The ground floor has rusticated masonry, the first floor has balustrades below the windows and, typically Carr, there is a half-storey above.

The hall was once visited by the two Lord Byrons, father and son, who were both rumoured to have run off with the lady of the manor on separate occasions. Byron junior, the famous poet, took his lover to his residence at Newstead Abbey, but she was soon dispatched back to Aston. An extant Byron letter, written from Aston Hall, encapsulates the poet's demise:

> It is three in the morning, and I can not rest, but I must try. I have been at Newstead and between that and this, my mind is at a stage of chaotic inaction; but you won't pity me, and I do not deserve it. Was there ever such a slave to impulse?

Site: Aston Hall is a country house hotel in the old village of Aston, just off the A57, about half a mile (0.8km) west of junction 31 of the M1.

Grid Ref: SK 469852 (Landranger 111, Pathfinder 744)

Kiveton's Lost Mansion

Reused gate piers and the end sections of two outbuildings are almost all that remains of Kiveton House or Hall. Demolished in 1811 after little more than a century of occupation, it was once one of the most fashionable houses in the North of England.

Badeslade's engraving of about 1730 displays a showpiece two-storey front of eleven bays, with a central entrance framed by four giant pilasters crowned by a triangular pediment enclosing a coat of arms. Connecting wings faced a square courtyard separated from the park by an ornamental fence or screen (not unlike the recently restored example at Hampton Court), the work of Jean Tijou, the foremost decorative metalworker of the age. The house and park was developed for one of the most powerful aristocrats and politicians of the Williamite court, Thomas Osborne, whose long list of titles included that of earl of Danby, marquis of Carmarthen and first duke of Leeds. The duke could afford to commission the best craftsmen in England and Europe to furnish the interior.

Site: the gate piers are at the entrance to Kiveton Hall Farm, and can be seen from Kiveton Lane, between Todwick and Kiveton.

Grid Ref: SK 498835 (Landranger 111, Pathfinder 744)

A Font for all Seasons

Enter the small church of St Peters at Thorpe Salvin and you will see an exceptionally fine piece of Norman craftsmanship. The font here is one of the best examples of its kind in the country.

The shape is cylindrical, with beaded arches and a wavy band of stylised leaves at the top; but its main decoration consists of a series of five carved scenes. The ceremony of baptism is a common Norman subject. The other images are of the seasons, represented by sowing (spring), riding under the shade of the tree (summer), reaping or binding corn (autumn) and a man warming his feet by a the fire (winter). In a further scene, the carver has reproduced the form of a human face with a zigzag design emanating from its mouth. The remaining face of the font has no figurative carving, instead a series of intersecting arches.

Site: Thorpe Salvin is about twelve miles (19km) south-east of Rotherham and five miles (8km) of Worksop. The church is normally locked but a key can be obtained locally.

Grid Ref: SK 521812 (Landranger 111, Pathfinder 744)

Elizabethan Splendour at Thorpe Salvin

The exterior stonework of the south front are all that remains of the fine Elizabethan house of the Sandfords, but the corner towers, projecting bays and massive chimney stacks make it an impressive ruin. Entrance was via an attractive two-storeyed gatehouse with stepped gables, a coat of arms just visible over its wide doorway. The ruin, once at risk of complete demolition, is now protected by English Heritage and is listed as a grade II (starred) historic building.

After the death of Hercy Sandford in 1586, the house passed to the Neviles of Chevet, near Wakefield, who sold to Sir Edward Osborne of Kiveton, whose illustrious second son, Thomas, became the first duke of Leeds. For many years the hall was occupied by tenants, the Osbornes having abandoned Thorpe in favour of a brand-new mansion at Kiveton (see page 50) but the old house, albeit ruinous, has outlived its fashionable rival. The house has literary associations: 'Torquilstone' in Sir Walter Scott's novel Ivanhoe is thought to be based on Thorpe Salvin Hall.

Site: the ruin can be viewed from Lady Field Road, Thorpe Salvin.

Grid Ref: SK522813 (Landranger 111, Pathfinder 744)

Fretwell's 'Dutch' house

The future of Hellaby Hall was in serious doubt during the early 1980s, its exceptional Jacobean façade, completed in 1692, in danger of complete collapse. Vacated in 1976, a fire had destroyed much of the interior. Local construction company Frewvale bought the hall estate and, with the help of English Heritage, began the expensive restoration process and conversion to a hotel. The hotel closed after a few months and the building remained empty for a further four years. However, its doors reopened in 1995 as a prestigious four-star hotel by Tomorrows Leisure.

The old hall was built for Ralph Fretwell, a local man who made his fortune planting sugar in Barbados, where he had seen houses built in the Dutch style. Fretwell even shipped horses from his Hellaby estate to turn the mill machinery that crushed the sugar cane. He is also believed to have owned a large part of Philadelphia, and was appointed as chief justice of the Court of Common Pleas in Barbados, but was dismissed for his Quaker beliefs, having offended the Establishment by allowing Negroes to attend religious meetings in his house. Returning to Hellaby in 1688, he began work on his new house using the very best Roche stone, its spectacular gable with its spiral scrolls a real eyecatcher. He returned alone to Barbados, where he died in 1701, and remains one of South Yorkshire's pioneering but enigmatic entrepreneurs.

Site: Old Hellaby Lane, off the A631 (Bawtry) road, between Rotherham and Maltby, near junction 1 of the M18.

Grid Ref: SK 506923 (Landranger 111, Pathfinder 727)

Barnsley and Beyond

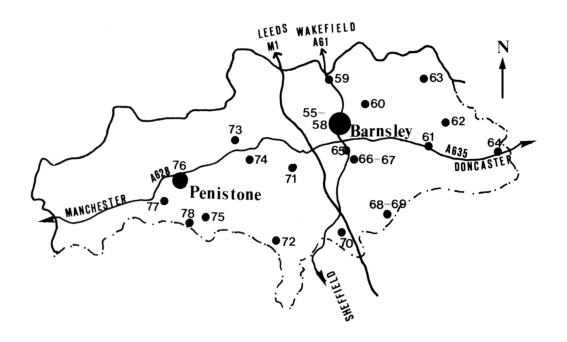

The Colliers' Metropolis

The miners' union headquarters is one of Barnsley's most famous buildings. The sender of an Edwardian picture postcard inscribed 'The Collier's Metropolis' under its image. More recently, elements of the media have referred to it as 'Arthur's Castle' or 'Camelot' because of its associations with Arthur Scargill.

The building opened in 1874, as headquarters of the-then sixteen year old South Yorkshire Miners' Association. At the national conference, held here a few days after the official opening, miners' secretary John Normansell spoke with great pride about the new union premises. It was not, he said, 'for himself [and other miners' leaders] but for the miners, their children, and their children's children'. He went on to describe its 'cheerful and pleasant appearance' in contrast to some of the dreadful working conditions, injuries and loss of life that wrecked so many mining families. The wholesale closure of pits following the 1984-5 strike — as predicted by the union — has resulted in a great reduction in working miners, yet the office continues to serve about the same number of members as it did in its infancy, over a century ago.

Site: the corner of Huddersfield Road and Victoria Road, central Barnsley.

Grid Ref: SE 342068 (Landranger 111, Pathfinder 715)

'We Supply all but the Baby'

Nowadays it is difficult for small family retailers to compete with large stores and shopping centres. It is also rare for small shops to remain in the same family for several generations. Bailey's, situated almost opposite the main entrance to Barnsley's prestigious Alhambra Centre, was an exceptional survivor.

This family concern had been associated with children's and women's fashion for over a century. Edward Bailey opened his drapery emporium on Cheapside in 1883, and his distinctive sign 'We Supply all but the Baby' soon became a popular landmark. The use of a stork above the slogan was a cunning piece of advertising. Bailey's had business interests in the town for several years before establishing their well-earned reputation. The business was relocated to its present site in 1968 and even survived the building of the Alhambra Shopping Centre, but it was an emotional day in July 1997 when Jean Bailey, seventy-four, retired and the shop finally closed its doors. The famous stork sign, though, has been given a new nesting place at Elsecar Heritage Centre.

Site: 5 New Street, Barnsley.

*Grid Ref: SE 348063
(Landranger 111,
Pathfinder 715)*

The Leaning Tower of Barnsley

Mining subsidence and the drought of 1995 has played havoc with one of Barnsley's most spectacular listed buildings. The observation tower in Locke Park was presented to the town in 1877, funded by Sarah McCreery, as a memorial to her late sister, Phoebe, widow of the great railway engineer Joseph Locke who spent his formative years in Barnsley. It was built by Robinson and Son, a local firm to the design of the Paris architect R Renee Spiers.

For many years sightseers have been barred — in the interests of safety — from ascending the tower and sampling the views from the observation balcony. By February 1996 the tower was twenty-two inches (56cm) askew, though not in immediate danger of falling down. Council officials are pinning their hopes on cash from the Millennium Commission in order to carry out repairs and make the building accessible to the public once again.

Site: Locke Park, Barnsley.

Grid Ref: SE 342051 (Landranger 111, Pathfinder 715)

For Brass Bands in the Park

A crowd of 25,000 attended the grand opening of the new Locke Park bandstand in 1908 and were treated to a rousing performance from the Barnsley Volunteers' Band.

In every town and in many villages of South Yorkshire, brass bands had become an integral part of community spirit. The competitive aspect of performance was an essential musical motivation, but bands also loved to show off their repertoire in open-air settings, none better than in public parks where ornamental stands were the perfect bases for Sunday concerts in the summer. Brass bands were in such demand during the late Victorian and Edwardian period that pattern-book bandstands were available to order from the catalogues of ironmasters. The Barnsley park bandstand was commissioned from the Lion Foundry Company of Kirkintilloch and cost £326. Over the years it has lost some of its original ironwork, yet still retains a typical eastern appearance.

Site: in Locke Park, Barnsley, which can be accessed from either Park Road or Keresforth Hall Road, about a mile (1.6km) from the centre of town.

Grid Ref: SE 340053

A Monastic Logo

The once-extensive area served by the ancient parish church at Royston included the townships of Cudworth, Monk Bretton, Carlton, Notton, Chevet, Royston itself, and distant Woolley which had a chapel-of-ease.

Not surprisingly, the medieval church of St John the Baptist is a substantial building, especially the fifteenth century tower which continues to be a striking landmark. Its most curious feature is an attractive oriel window (very rare indeed for parish churches) projecting from the walls, set between the belfry and the west window. The heraldic shields and covered unguent pots under each light relate to the Benedictine monks of the priory of St Mary Magdalene of Lund ('Monk Bretton Priory'), who would have installed the window, since they were responsible for the maintenance of the church and its services. It has been suggested that the oriel served as a candle- and/or lantern-lit chamber for prayer and meditation, appreciated by travellers at night; but, more importantly, it was a symbolic and very obvious reminder to ordinary people of monastic ownership.

Site: Church Street, Royston, three miles (5km) north-east of Barnsley.

Grid Ref: SK 364112 (Landranger 110 or 111, Pathfinder 703)

The Mill of the Black Monks

This ancient cornmill, once associated with the twelfth century Monk Bretton Priory, was opened as a public house and restaurant in 1991, and named Mill of the Black Monks — after the Benedictines who were 'in residence' from 1281 until 1538. The conversion process was the culmination of eight years' work by architect Malcolm Lister, including the considerable engineering feat of raising the structure almost six feet (2m) in order to solve the persistent problem of flooding.

After the Dissolution the building continued to grind corn under Crown ownership, and was generally known as the 'Abbey Mill'. It was the subject of litigation in 1638 when William Silvester, a Quaker, who rented the mill for five nobles (a gold coin worth 6s 8d) per annum, was accused by the powerful Sir Francis Wortley, owner of mills in Barnsley, of grinding considerable amounts of Barnsley corn (and therefore taking trade from his mills). Old people in the locality appeared as witnesses. The case appears to have fallen through due to recollections that proved a custom of carrying Barnsley corn to the Abbey Mill had been established sixty years earlier.

The mill was probably rebuilt in the mid-seventeenth century under the auspicies of Lady Mary Armine, neice of Gilbert Talbot, seventh earl of Shrewsbury, but many features have been retained in a sympathetic restoration, rightly recognised by a Civic Trust award in 1992.

Site: east of Barnsley, on Grange Lane (A633), Cundy Cross, by the River Dearne.
Grid Ref: SK 372063 (Landranger 110, Pathfinder 715)

A Black Obelisk
for a Black Day

At the south-eastern edge of
the old churchyard at Darfield
stands a grim reminder of one
of the most tragic mining
disasters of Victorian Barnsley.
An explosion of fire-damp
blasted through the underground workings of the new
Lundhill Colliery, near Wombwell, on a cold February day in
1857, causing the deaths of
189 men and boys. The
explosion sent tremors above
ground over many hundreds of
yards and tremors in the hearts
of hundreds of local people.
The disaster had the dubious
accolade of front-page cover-
age in the prestigious *Illustrated London News*, a 'first'
for a mining tragedy. The
Kellett family lost five sons.
Such events had voyeuristic
appeal, attracting 'coach loads
of excursionists'. It was estimated that a crowd of 15,000
assembled at the pit head,
many of them in a jocular
mood, though a few sang
hymns. Two years later Charles
Dickens was with a party of
'literary men' who toured some
of the workings of the stricken
pit.

Site: All Saints churchyard, Darfield, six miles (9.5km) east of Barnsley.
Grid Ref: SE 418043 (Landranger 111, Pathfinder 716)

Sir Edward Rodes's Chapel

The Rodes family were noted Nonconformists, their fine Elizabethan house at Great Houghton a focus for Presbyterian dissenters. In about 1650 Sir Edward Rodes (whose sister was the third wife of Thomas Wentworth, earl of Strafford, Charles I's chief minister, who was executed in 1641) built a chapel in the grounds of his hall. There was a succession of dissenting ministers, culminating in Nathanial Denton who died, aged eighty-seven, in 1720. At the Archbishop's Visitation in 1743 the chapel was described as 'united to the Church of England'.

Now dedicated to St Michael and All Hallows, it has unusual rounded, crow-stepped gables and curved 'battlements', a distinctive sight near modern housing. The soft sandstone has worn by age and atmospheric pollution, the family crest having

disintegrated. Inside there is a Puritan pulpit and box pews. A Royalist force attacked and plundered the hall during the Civil War, ill-treating the lady of the house, killing a servant and wounding another. Converted to an inn, the old hall was gutted by fire in 1960 and subsequently demolished. A modern public house now occupies part of the site. The chapel remains as an interesting historic building and is still used for services.

Site: the junction of Church Street and Rodes Avenue (off High Street),
Great Houghton, about seven miles (11km) east of Barnsley.

Grid Ref: SE 430065 (Landranger 110, Pathfinder 716)

Brassed Off

The sod-cutting ceremony at Grimethorpe took place in October 1894, amid complaints from the Badsworth Hunt that the best part of its 'country' would be lost. The *Barnsley Chronicle*'s prediction of a 'sleepy village' suddenly transformed into a busy centre of population soon materialised, whilst Joseph Mitchell, the new pit's managing director, anticipated 2,500 tons a day. The colliery was the life-blood of the village, employing at least one member of most families.

Michael Heseltine's parliamentary announcement on the future of the coal industry in June 1992 was soon followed by British Coal's intention to close thirty pits in preparation for privatisation. Despite many protests, 'Grimey' closed on Friday the 7th May 1993, its 959 workforce having dwindled via enhanced redundancies to a few stalwarts.

Halves of the pit headgear wheel were subsequently placed in the village, one appropriately next to the entrance to Willowgarth High School. *Energy is Coal — The Grimethorpe Pit Closure* was produced on an October day when pupils, staff and local people expressed their feelings about the pits's ninety-eight year history and a copy was delivered to 10 Downing Street. The Acorn Centre and a regeneration plan may give new hope to the area. Famous for its colliery brass band, Grimethorpe was recently featured in the acclaimed film *Brassed Off* (1996).

Site: Brierley Road, Grimethorpe.

Grid Ref: SE 411103 (Landranger111, Pathfinder 716)

The First Concrete Church

Today the tower of St John the Evangelist and St Mary at Goldthorpe is a distinctive landmark, especially prominent from the new bypass. Built during the middle years of the Great War and costing £23,000, it was the first church substantially constructed of concrete in the country. This interesting building replaced St Alban's Mission, or the 'Tin Tab', which had served a burgeoning mining community for twenty years.

Its unusual appearance and design owes much to the influence of Lord Halifax, who lived nearby at Hickleton Hall, and his architect Alfred Nutt. That both men, aged seventy-seven and sixty-nine respectively, chose such a new building material may seem surprising. However, concrete provided a relatively quick and economic means of completing the work, whilst the light exterior and interior contrasted with the dark, underground world of the miners, 'more inspiring and elevating that what is likely to result from their ordinary surroundings'. What was not appreciated in 1916 was the long-term effect of atmospheric pollution and the corrosion of exposed steel rods on the fabric.

Site: Lockwood Road, off Doncaster Road (B6098), Goldthorpe.

Grid Ref: SE 464046 (Landranger 111, Pathfinder 716)

'The dark round of the dripping wheel ...' (Tennyson)

A mill was recorded at Worsbrough by the *Domesday* commissioners. We can not be certain if the present mill, whose oldest parts date from the seventeenth century, occupies the same site as its medieval predecessors, though the River Dove provided a successful location. Processing cereals from surrounding farms, the mill was an essential part of the rural economy. It became part of the estate of the Edmunds family of Worsbrough Hall.

Although the mill was made more productive by the use of steam power (and later oil), it could not match the output of the new rolling mills or indeed the demand for white bread. The old mill continued to work, though spasmodically, until the 1960s. The Old and New Mill were rescued from dereliction through the campaigns of Mr A O Elmhirst and other enthusiasts, eventually restored by the former West Riding and South Yorkshire county councils. After local government reorganisation, the mill complex and country park were taken over by Barnsley Council. The mill now functions as a popular working museum and excellent educational resource. Traditional flours are still produced.

Site: three miles (5km) south of Barnsley, off the Barnsley–Sheffield (A61) road. The main entrance, leading to a large car park, is almost opposite the Red Lion Inn. The museum is open Wed–Sun & Bank Holiday Mondays 10am–5pm (4pm winter)

Grid Ref: SE 349033 (Landranger 111, Pathfinder 715)

Mind t' Causey!

From medieval times to the nineteenth century, lines of flagstones or 'causeys' were laid along routeways to combat the problems associated with the wearing away of trackways. They were particularly useful on wet, sloping and slippery land, enabling horses to traverse difficult terrain. 'Mind t' causey edge!' was an expression often directed at the writer when he was a young boy by an anxious mother, anticipating (often correctly) a potential trip or fall. The word is still used in local speech.

A number of important packhorse routeways passed through Barnsley, and short stretches of causeways still survive in the Kingstone and Worsbrough areas, not far from the town centre. Causeys are mentioned in wills and a variety of other records, but on the ground are difficult to date with any certainty. The local place-name 'Stairfoot', where four roads descend to meet at a busy roundabout, was probably a good example of a stepped causey. It is pleasing that this example has not gone the way of most others: removed or lost under a covering of tarmac.

Site: the upper (south) side of Hound Hill Lane, near to the junction with Genn Lane, between Kingstone and Ward Green.

Grid Ref: SE 339044 (Landranger 111, Pathfinder 715)

A Bunk-bed Monument

Enter St Mary's Church, Worsbrough, and you will see a most remarkable two-tier monument. Made mainly of oak, with an effigy on each bunk, it commemorates a local knight, Roger Rockley, who died in 1533 aged about thirty-five. The upper representation consists of a delicately-carved handsome figure of a young knight in armour, his hands in a position of prayer and his eyes gazing, appreciatively, heavenwards. In great contrast, below is the same figure after death, in the form of a shrouded cadaver or skeleton, resting on a tomb chest which has part-painted armoural shields (of Rockley and Mounteney), carved in relief and arranged in five panels. The sixteenth century craftsman had covered the timber effigies with strips of linen which were then painted, in order to simulate reality. In his will of 1522, Sir Roger Rockley provided gifts to maidens and single men married at Worsbrough during the seven years after his death; and also for a continuance of hospitality to travellers for fifteen years after his decease.

Site: south side of the chancel in St Mary's Church, Worsbrough village.

Grid Ref: SE 350026 (Landranger 110, Pathfinder 715)

Earl Fitzwilliam's Very Own Railway Station

A private railway station was opened at Elsecar in 1870 for the convenience of Earl Fitzwilliam, who lived in the great house at Wentworth two miles (3km) away. The arrival and departure of the earl and his guests caused understandable interest from local children, according to one recollection, recorded in 1972:

> *Everyone flocked to see the Fitzwilliam coaches arrive at the special platform at Elsecar, driven by coachmen in yellow and black liveries. There was a scramble as the occupants showered us with Doncaster butterscotch as they returned [from Doncaster Races].*

In the waiting room the noble party were served with refreshments and could board in total privacy. The large doorway was where the railway passed through the building. Today the Fitzwilliam Station houses the Elsecar People exhibition, part of the Elsecar Discovery Centre.

Site: Elsecar is eight miles (13km) south of Barnsley. Follow the brown 'Elsecar Heritage' signs from all main routes. The main entrance is via Wentworth Road, where there is a large car park.

Grid Ref: SK 388999 (Landranger 111, Pathfinder 726)

Saved!

Many South Yorkshire buildings of historic and architectural merit have been lost in the postwar era, even in so-called conservation areas. An interesting exception can be seen at Elsecar. Today Fitzwilliam Lodge is a fine-looking three-storey structure, sympathetically restored and refurbished for domestic usage. By 1980, through a combination of neglect and vandalism, the abandoned building, with boarded and broken windows, missing roof slates and decaying stonework, was at risk of complete demolition.

It was commissioned by Earl Fitzwilliam in the early 1850s as a lodging house for single miners, but his lordship may have overestimated the need for such accommodation, young men often preferring to live at home with parents. By 1862, after many months of being empty, it was supposedly to be converted to a school, but in about 1870 was used a police station and two cottages. Later

it was known as the 'Bun and Milk Club', where alcoholic drinks were barred. In 1983 a housing association — with support from Barnsley Metropolitan Borough Council planning department — saw its potential and converted it into desirable flats, a good example of funding an historic building in a viable but non-damaging way.

Site: Fitwilliam Street, Elsecar, opposite Armroyd Lane.

Grid Ref: SE 383003 (Landranger 110, Pathfinder 715)

Tankersley Old Hall

Although the Old Hall in Tankersley Park is now a ruin, architectural features such as fireplaces and mullioned and transomed windows give some impression of its former grandeur.

The Elizabethan house was probably occupied by the Savile family from the beginning of the sixteenth century, a fashionable residence set within what was a medieval deer park. In the 1630s Thomas Wentworth, the ill-fated earl of Strafford and new owner of the hall, made one of the Rockley family, a cousin, master of game in his park, with instructions to keep the mansion in good repair. The Old Hall survived the Civil War, despite an alleged battle at 'Tankersley Moor', and was leased by Sir Richard Fanshaw as country seat. When Defoe visited the park in the 1720s he was impressed by the size of the deer, one of the hinds 'bigger than my horse'. The park was subsequently transformed into a more picturesque setting by the marquis of Rockingham, who lived in the huge house and landscaped park at Wentworth Woodhouse, and the Old Hall began to decay. The ruin was the location of a scene in Ken Loache's 1970 film *Kes* (based on local author Barry Hines's book *Kestrel for a Knave*) when young Billy Casper (Dai Bradley) climbed the wall to obtain his kestrel.

Site: about six miles (9.5km) south of Barnsley. Follow the minor road (Church Lane) and track past St Peter's Church, Tankersley. The hall is on private property and unsafe for close viewing, but can be seen from the bridleway.

Grid Ref: SK 356988 (Landranger 111, Pathfinder 715)

Baroque splendour at Northern College

The Northern College (for residential adult education) is housed in one of the most magnificent mansions in the North of England and is surrounded by the only Grade 1 listed landscape in South Yorkshire.

The great house was the home of a branch of the medieval lords of Wentworth, who had built a house — which became known as Wentworth Woodhouse — near the village from which they had taken their surname. The Stainborough estate was purchased in 1708 by Thomas Wentworth, whose title of Lord Raby had passed from his illustrious uncle, the first earl of Strafford; but Wentworth was outraged at being overlooked in favour of his cousin and namesake (soon to be known as Thomas Watson-Wentworth) who had inherited the family seat at Wentworth.

The Stainborough estate gave Raby chance to redress the balance, but in reality was the start of years of family rivalry. His first act was to commission Berlin architect Jean de Bodt to design a new east range at Stainborough. The exterior was completed in 1713 under the supervision of Thomas Archer, one of the best of the new Baroque architects. In 1711, Queen Anne made Raby the first earl of Strafford of the second creation, and his marriage to a wealthy heiress a year later ensured that he was able to furnish his new house and create a grand garden in the most fashionable of styles.

Site: Lowe Lane, Stainborough, about three miles (5km) south-west of Barnsley. Leave the M1 via junction 37 (from north) or junction 36 (from south).

Grid Ref: SK 320032 (Landranger 110, Pathfinder 715)

A Unique Industrial Legacy

Before the large-scale development of industry, a series of water-powered heavy forges were sited along the River Don and its larger tributaries. The Top Forge, once part of the Wortley Ironworks, is a unique example and is of national importance. Its preservation, maintenance, conversion to a public museum and continued restoration is a tribute to past and present members of the South Yorkshire Industrial History Society and its trust. The site includes a dam, sluices and water wheels, and houses two water-powered tilt hammers with hand-powered cranes. The museum is of considerable educational importance and attracts many visitors when steam days and special events are held.

The forge dates from the 1620s when it was established by Sir Francis Wortley, but by the early eighteenth century had become a part of a gentry ironworking partnership, lead by John Spencer of Cannon Hall *(see opposite)*. The most notable early

'managers' were Matthew Wilson (whose initials are carved on a 1713 datestone) and the Cockshutt family. The second John Cockshutt patented a method for making iron direct from ore and was a pioneer of the local wiremaking trade, using steel drawing plates, whilst his brother James, a fellow of the Royal Society, was one of the first to put into practice Henry Cort's puddling furnace for the making of wrought iron, invented in 1784. Railway axles were made here from 1835 until the closure of the forge in 1908.

Site: Cote Lane/Forge Lane, about half a mile (0.8km) south of Thurgoland, just off the A629; also via Finkle Street, Wortley and Soughley Lane (A616 Stocksbridge bypass). Open to the public on Sundays and by special arrangement.

Grid Ref: SK 294998 (Landranger 110, Pathfinder 726)

Picturesque Parkland and Home-grown Pineapples

Visitors to Barnsley are often surprised by the presence of attractive countryside and pleasant villages a short distance from the town. This is especially true at Cawthorne, with its medieval church and an abundance of historic buildings. Its most unusual asset is the Victoria Jubilee Museum, run by a committee of trustees on behalf of the people of the village, whilst Cannon Hall, an elegant former country house set in a landscaped park, attracts many visitors.

The hall was the ancestral home of the Spencer family and largely the creation of John Spencer, described in 1760 as a 'gentleman of modest means' but also a leading figure in the local iron industry. Spencer had both the vision and means to employ Richard Woods, a professional landscape gardener and nurseryman from Essex, and the famous York-based architect John Carr.

During the 1760s Woods completed design contracts for lakes, cascades, a palladian bridge and, closer to the house itself, a new ornamental garden, kitchen garden and even a hot house for pineapple plants. Meanwhile, Carr had completed his plans for the house, and 'busy planting' soon gave way to 'at home all day amongst the workmen' in Spencer's diary. There were three later phases of building by Carr, and it is a tribute to his ability that he completed a house that combined domestic utility and convenience with plain but pleasing proportions.

Site: Cawthorne is about four miles (6.5km) west of Barnsley just off the A635. The Cannon Hall Museum and County Park is open throughout the year, but visitors to the house should check opening times, especially between Christmas and New Year. The Jubilee Museum opens at weekend afternoons April–October, and by special arrangement.

Grid Ref: SK 272083 (Landranger 110, Pathfinder 715)

A Pit Tragedy

On a hot and sultry day in July 1838 a violent thunderstorm battered the countryside around Silkstone. A stream which ran by the entrance to the nearby Husker pit became a raging torrent, just as the workers were walking out of the drift. Doors held back the rushing water for a short time, but when there was an attempt by those inside to open them, they were swept aside by a wave of overwhelming force. The water subsided as quickly as it had risen, leaving behind the bodies of twenty-six children and young adults. Thirteen of the victims were girls, three as young as eight or nine. They were buried in seven graves, the girls at the feet of the boys, the oldest aged sixteen, the youngest seven.

This memorial, in a corner of Silkstone churchyard, marks the site of their

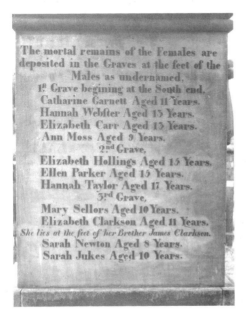

graves, a sad reminder of a terrible event that caused so much suffering to this small South Yorkshire village. The Husker Pit disaster was a very important factor leading to the establishment of a royal commission which resulted in the Act of 1842 stopping the employment underground of women and girls, and boys under the age of ten years.

Site: by the wall on the west side of All Saints churchyard, Silkstone.

Grid Ref: SE 290058 (Landranger 110, Pathfinder 715)

Willow Bridge

The tinkling of bells was once a familiar sound in the attractive wooded valley of the Don downstream from Penistone, on the ancient route between Bradfield and Wakefield. The bells were attached to the collar of a leading horse, guided by an attendant or 'jagger', and warned of the approach of a string of packhorses as they crossed the Don via Willow Bridge.

Dating from about 1734, the humped-back bridge has low parapets which reduced contact with laden panniers strapped to the backs of small but sturdy and sure-footed horses. Packhorses were the juggernauts of the pre-turnpike era, carrying produce

such as salt, cheese and potatoes over the Pennines and into the West Riding, returning laden with hemp, flax and yarn. Industrial products were also carried to and from, for example, nearby Wortley Forge *(see page 72)*.

Site: Willow Bridge, Sheffield Road, Oxspring; follow the bridleway opposite St Aiden's church for about 350 yards (320m).

Grid Ref: SE 267026 (Landranger 110, Pathfinder 715)

The Cloth Hall

The building in Penistone market place, now occupied by Clarks chemist shop, was erected as a cloth hall in 1763. The local textile trade must have been of sufficient commercial potential for subscribers, headed by Josias Wordsworth, to risk £800, a considerable sum, in the project.

The market at Penistone had been established in 1699, despite opposition from leading traders in Barnsley. For generations a coarse, hard-wearing broadcloth was produced in the Penistone area and made into everyday clothes. A moorland breed of sheep, called Penistones, was named after the town, as was the distinctive local cloth.

The architect entrusted with the design of the Cloth Hall was John Platt, who had had recent experience of a shambles and market place commission in Doncaster (and a later one in Barnsley). The large shop windows would have been open arches leading into the Market House and Cloth Hall. Unfortunately the cloth trade didn't prosper, the entire block being sold for £615 in 1825, and by 1851 it had become the White Bear pub. Its most famous occupant was postmaster John Wood, who produced the *Penistone Almanack* and for many years helped stage the Penistone Show.

Site: market place, Penistone.

Grid Ref: SE 247033 (Landranger 110, Pathfinder 715)

The Dissenters' Chapel

After the Restoration many Puritan vicars and rectors were ejected from their livings, but this was not the case in Penistone where minor gentry families continued to support Reverend Henry Swift, who refused to use the official prayer book and to wear the surplice. Swift's death, in 1689, allowed the Crown to appoint a successor with Conformist views, but Elkanah Rich, who had registered his hall as a meeting place for Protestant dissenters, decided to build a chapel in the grounds. Bullhouse Independent Chapel was completed in April 1692. Its first pastor was Daniel Denton MA, who received a grant of £20 per annum, his keep and a horse; and lived in a tiny cottage at the rear of the building. In 1715 the congregation, despite the chapel's modest size and remote setting, numbered 200.

An annual performance of Handel's *Messiah*, a tradition which began in 1926, attracts many former members, and the chapel is once more packed to capacity. The interior has fine oak panelling and a magnificent original pulpit. The whole chapel continues to be well-cared for, a tremendous tribute to its small regular congregation.

Site: two miles (3km) west of Thurlstone; access is via a minor road (Bullhouse Lane) off the A628 (Manchester) road at Bullhouse railway bridge, or a footpath/bridleroad to Bullhouse Mill via the B6106. Please note that Bullhouse Hall is private property.

Grid Ref: SE 211027 (Landranger 110, Pathfinder 715)

An Essential Guide

High above Stocksbridge — in a corner of a field near where four roads meet — is a stone pillar, not unlike a gatepost. Closer inspection reveals a more important usage. It is in fact a guide stoop or waymarker for travellers.

This unusual hexagonal example would have been erected, as was the custom, by order of the West Riding justices of the peace and is dated 1734. It lies on a lonely upland part of the ancient saltway route linking Cheshire, via Woodhead, to Wakefield or Doncaster, and was a vital aid in such a remote and sparsely populated district. Direction was ascertained by turning *right* of the inscription: for example, the traveller would go to the right when facing the side marked 'Sheffield & Rotterham [sic]'. The five other sides are inscribed:

Barnsley and Pontefract 1734
Doncaster

Wakefield and Leeds

Penistone, Huthersfield [sic]
and Hallifax

Woodhead and Mottram

Underbank and Bradfield

Like causeys *(see page 66)* and packhorse bridges *(see page 75)*, such features bear witness to the increasing volume of traffic (especially relating to trade) in this period.

Site : Dyson Cote Lane, near the junction with Salter Hill–Tofts Lane and Underbank Lane, one mile (1.6km) north-west of Stocksbridge and two miles (3km) south of Penistone.

Grid Ref: SK258004 (Landranger 110, Pathfinder 726)

In and Around Doncaster

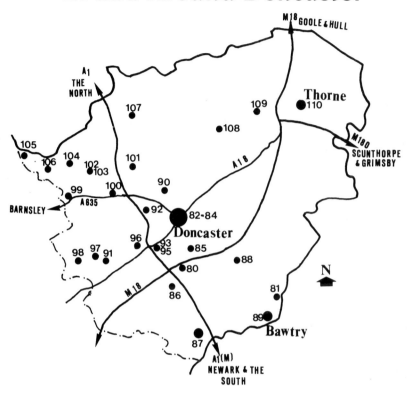

Patterns in Stone

The tomb-chest in the churchyard at Loversall serves as an unusual example of late medieval stone-carving. Its south side in particular has been inscribed with a variety of tracery design, as though the mason wanted to show off his skill. Here we can see patterns in Y-tracery, intersected tracery (cusped and uncusped), and two- and three-light window openings. Perhaps he was copying the designs from a standard book of patterns. The tomb has a weathered foliated cross on the lid.

The small church, dedicated to St Katherine, was subjected to considerable Victorian alteration, but the interior houses two medieval monuments as well as other interesting features. Thankfully bypassed by a main road, the old village of Loversall has several historic buildings, including a hall and seventeenth century dovecote.

Site: Loversall is about three miles (5km) south of Doncaster. The church is in a pleasant location, behind farm buildings and reached via an avenue of trees. The tomb-chest lies south of the south chapel.

Grid Ref: SK 576987 (Landranger 111, Pathfinder 727)

The Dragon of Austerfield

Enter the porch of the small Norman church of St Helena at Austerfield, and one's eye is drawn to a doorway with an arch carved in typical zigzag and beak-head style. The appearance is not as grand as Fishlake (see page 109), but the tympanum — the space between the lintel and the arch above it — contains a most unusual feature. Here we can see a crude representation of what appears to be a serpent or dragon with a tail resembling an arrowhead. The lintel itself is decorated with a band of semi-circular merlons (raised 'battlements') above a line of partly damaged paterae (circular design) and rosettes. St Helena receives many American visitors because of its association with the most famous Pilgrim Father, William Bradford, who was baptised here in 1590.

Site: Austerfield is situated just off the main A638 road between Bawtry and Doncaster, about one and a half miles (2.5km) from Bawtry on the A614.

Grid Ref: SK 662947 (Landranger 111, Pathfinder 728)

Civic Splendour

A long succession of Doncaster mayors have been able to entertain their guests in the finest civic building in the county. The Mansion House, one of only three in the country (the others being at York and London), was the commission of the Palladian architect James Paine. The work, estimated at more than £4,500, took three years to complete, the building officially opening on the 15th April 1749.

A predictable feature of Paine's design was the large central Venetian window, with four symmetrically placed pairs of Corinthian columns gracing the street front, each capital decorated with acanthus leaves; but the recessed ground floor entrance, through rusticated stonework, is an unusual feature. The construction of two wings was abandoned. Paine's reputation was such that he was also working nearby at Cusworth, Wadworth and Hickleton. An attic storey was added in 1801, to the design of local man William Lindley.

Site: High Street, Doncaster.

Grid Ref: SE 574033 (Landranger 111, Pathfinder 716)

Elite Betting Rooms

The pillared portico of the 'Subscription Rooms', designed by Messrs Woodhead and Hurst in 1826 and built on a prime site close to the Mansion House, are all that remains of Doncaster's most exclusive club. Members, who paid a guinea a year, could socialise in relaxed and comfortable surroundings, especially during race week when no doubt substantial bets were waged. Paganini, the famous Italian violinist and composer — who had a reputation for mesmerising audiences (especially females) — gave a concert here in 1833.

The rooms' popularity declined, the target of much criticism and even constabular intervention during the anti-gambling climate of the Victorian period; but the building continued to be used for a variety of purposes: as a dance academy, furniture warehouse, and even a cinema. Today the façade is earmarked as a frontispiece of a new shopping mall, subject to planning permission.

Site: High Street, Doncaster.

Grid Ref: SE 575034 (Landranger 111, Pathfinder 716)

Skeletons in the Market Place

Shortly after the writer took this photograph, in January 1994, the famous Corn Exchange in the market place, one of Doncaster's most important public buildings, was seriously damaged by fire.

Completed in 1875 to the design of William Watkins, its original agricultural function diversified as a venue for concerts and large public meetings; and latterly as an indoor market. Inside, the decorated ironwork and glass provided ample evidence of quality Victorian craftsmanship and engineering.

Internal refurbishment work included the construction of a new floor level, which gave opportunity for an archaeological investigation, since the building was near the site of the ancient parish church of St Mary Magdalene. The public were able to watch the dig from a viewing gallery at the back of the indoor market. One trench contained five human skeletons from the medieval graveyard of St Mary's. Burial remains have been left *in situ* under the new floor, protected by a layer of sand and a specially-cast concrete slab.

Site: market place, Doncaster.

Grid Ref: SE 575034 (Landranger 111)

Planted by Sir David Attenborough

In 1993 a tree was planted by the famous broadcaster and naturalist Sir David Attenborough to mark the twenty-fifth anniversary of Potteric Carr Nature Reserve.

This area has long been associated with bog and marsh, the place-name 'Carr' associated with wetland habitats. The establishment of a duck decoy (with proceeds given to Doncaster's poor) was one early example of the use of the area by man. By

the end of the eighteenth century an effective drainage scheme, instigated by the well-known engineer John Smeaton, transformed the marsh into agricultural land. The subsequent impact of coalmining and the necessary railway infrastructure 'recreated' a subsided wetland habitat.

In 1968 the Yorkshire Wildlife Trust, realising the potential of the site, made an agreement with British Railways to manage the area as a nature reserve. The proximity of industry, housing, railway and motorway may appear an improbable setting but, in the words of the late Michael Clegg, it has become 'a magic place' for present and future generations to enjoy, a haven for a diverse variety of birds, fauna and flora. Wetland birds of Potteric Carr were featured on a set of Royal Mail stamps in 1996, the series launched by yet another television personality, Bill Oddie.

Site: three miles (5km) south of Doncaster, close to the M18 and A6182. Car park at Balby Carr. Access to the reserve is normally via day or annual permit; field centre and café open Tuesdays (March–Oct) and Sundays (all year).

Grid Ref: 5899 (Landranger 111, Pathfinder 716)

Dancing Merrily Around the Maypole

The tall red-and-white Maypole in the attractive village of Wadworth is a modern replacement of the older timber pole which can be seen featured on Edwardian picture postcards. Today the annual May dancing — probably in the interests of road safety —

is confined to the school playing field, but remains a rare example of the survival of an ancient village custom.

May Day once included the gathering of blossom from the hawthorn tree, a country tradition stretching way back to pre-Christian times. The Maypole, 'as high as the mast of a hundred ton vessel', was suspended with wreaths of flowers on May morning before the commencement of dancing and merriment. The Puritans caused many Maypoles to be taken down, but some were revived after 1660.

Site: Wadworth is about four miles (6.5km) south of Doncaster. The pole can be seen at the centre of the village, by the White Hart pub on Main Street (A60).

Grid Ref: SK 570969 (Landranger 111, Pathfinder 727)

An Elegant Butter Cross

The market or butter cross that graces the centre of Tickhill is the most elegant example in South Yorkshire. The plaque on its east face tells us that it was 'erected by the Reverend Christopher Alderson vicar of this parish about the year 1777'. and restored by his grand-daughter in 1898. The water pump commemorates Queen Victoria's diamond jubilee.

Tickhill was one of the most important settlements in medieval Yorkshire, its market place pre-dating royal licences. The area around the market is known as Sunderland, or 'land set aside for a special purpose', and may have originated because Sunderland Street was 'sundered' by the town's defensive ditch. With its Norman castle, magnificent perpendicular church and a wealth of historic buildings, Tickhill is a most handsome small country town.

Site: the centre of town, where the principal routes converge.

Grid Ref: SK 593934 (Landranger 111, Pathfinder 728)

An Historic Water Pump

Water supply has been the subject of considerable debate in the Yorkshire region in recent years. Our recent ancestors appeared to have survived droughts reasonably well, obtaining water from springs, wells, boreholes and via pumps.

This village pump at Rossington has survived and is a 'listed building'. The Gothic structure is surmounted by a short spire. Inside are mechanical remains: flywheel on a projecting axle, gear wheel and crank linked to a pump rod. There are no apparent leakages!

Site: Station Road, about fifty yards (45m) west of Stripe road, Rossington, which is five miles (8km) southeast of Doncaster.

Grid Ref: SK 623984 (Landranger 111, Pathfinder 728)

The Remnants of an Old Coaching Inn

Bawtry grew to prominence during the thirteenth and fourteenth centuries as a planned new town and inland port. Its fortunes declined in successive centuries, John Leland describing it as 'very bare and poore'. Trade revived during the seventeenth and eighteenth centuries due to improved navigation of the River Idle and carrier and coaching traffic on the Great North Road.

This eye-catching archway framed the entrance into the yard of the Angel Inn, a small posting house where horses were changed. Innholders often had other business interests, and this appears to have been the case with the Taylor family, proclaimed as 'Wine, Spirit & Seed Merchants'. The old inn has been converted into shops, but the advertising archway remains as an interesting reminder of one aspect of Bawtry's commercial past.

Site: in the market place, on the west side of High Street.

Grid Ref: SK 652931 (Landranger 111, Pathfinder 728)

Keeping Tally of Strays

Not long ago, most villages had pinfolds into which stray animals were placed and released on payment of a fine. The local official with responsibility for these small enclosures was known as a pinder, though often the village constable did the job. Traditionally, the pinder recorded the number of animals driven into the pinfold by cutting notches randomly spaced on a piece of wood about the size of a pencil, then splitting it lengthways. The keeper retained one half of the 'tally-stick', giving the other to the owner of the animal as receipt for payment of damages. Tally-sticks could not be forged as the notches had to coincide when the two parts were fitted together.

Where pinfolds survive intact they make interesting features. The Bentley pinfold is 'rectangular' with rounded corners, its walls of limestone rubble. Notice the narrow entrance and gate which would have had a lock. Contrasting examples can be seen at Bawtry and Wath-upon-Dearne. In 1608 a jury at Ecclesfield fined two locals for breaking into the pinfold there: 'Widowe Twigg' had to pay three shillings for the release of her impounded cattle, whilst Roger Milter was fined a similar sum 'for keeping a key to take his cattell out of the pinfoulde without leave'.

Site: Finkle Street, Bentley, three miles (5km) north of Doncaster.

Grid Ref: SE 569059 (Landranger 111, Pathfinder 716)

The King's Stronghold

When Sir Walter Scott visited Conisbrough in 1811, he was so impressed by the 'Saxon Fortress' that he used it as the setting for part of his romantic novel *Ivanhoe*.

The outstanding feature of the castle is its Norman circular keep, supported by six great buttresses. The white ashlar stone in remarkably good condition, making it one of the finest medieval military monuments in Europe. Conisbrough was held from 1163 to 1202 by Hamelin Plantagenet, who was half-brother of King Henry II. Later it became a royal castle when it passed to King Edward IV, but its decline had already began.

Although in the care of English Heritage, the castle is run by a charity — the Ivanhoe Trust — with the support of Doncaster Council. The partnership has resulted in EC and Government grants for major refurbishment: a new visitor centre, tea rooms and, most spectacularly, replacing the roof and floors of the keep. A state-of-the-art audio-visual presentation enhances the 'Conisbrough Experience'. The castle is now a major tourist and educational attraction, and a key feature in the regeneration of the Dearne Valley.

Site: north-east of Conisbrough town centre off the A630, four miles (6.5km) south-west of Doncaster. The castle is open Mon–Fri 10am–5pm, Sat–Sun 10am–6pm, in summer; and winter 10am–4pm.

Grid Ref: SK 515989 (Landranger 111, Pathfinder 727)

The Contrasting Façades of Cusworth Hall

Cusworth Hall was designed and begun in the early 1740s by George Platt, the Thrybergh mason-architect, and completed between 1743-5 by his sixteen year old son John. The Platts were master builders who always had close connections with quarries, Cusworth being a particularly suitable location because of a plentiful supply of local materials in the form of stone, plaster and lime.

The house was commissioned for the former MP for Newcastle-upon-Tyne, William Wrightson, who is supposed to have personally supervised the progress of the building from a bosun's chair attached to the scaffolding. The Platt/Wrightson north front, with its Venetian doorway and window, giant pilasters and curved flight of steps, has been preserved. However, in the early 1750s the south front *(illustrated)* was refaced by the fashionable architect James Paine, who also extended the frontage with the addition of two pavilions which served as chapel and library. The grounds were created in the naturalistic style by the landscape gardener Richard Woods of Chertsey, Surrey, who had worked at Cannon Hall *(see page 73)*. The grounds are open to the public, and the Hall, a grade I listed building, is now the Museum of South Yorkshire Life.

Site: Cusworth Lane (car park near gatehouse), two miles (3km) north-west Doncaster.
Grid Ref: SK 548038 (Landranger 111, Pathfinder 716)

'Very pretty for the size, but scarcely finished'

The 'manor, mansion house, lands and advowson' of Warmsworth was purchased from the heirs of the Bosville family by John Battie of Wadworth in April 1668. Before his death, in 1676, Battie appears to have made a start building a new house, for the hearth tax returns of 1672 record 12 hearths as against 8 in 1664. His son, also named John (1663–1724), carried out a major rebuilding in the early 1700s. Ralph Thoresby, the antiquary, described the house as 'very pretty for the size, but scarcely finished' in 1703.

And yet the projecting two-bay cross-wings of the south front (illustrated) are more in keeping with a much older plan. His son, a third John Battie, married Isabella — daughter of William Wrightson of Cusworth *(see opposite)* — in Sprotbrough Church in 1748, added 'Wrightson' to his surname and succeeded to the Cusworth estate. There began a close and long connection between the two halls, Warmsworth being rented by a succession of tenants. After almost thirty years of lying empty, the hall was purchased by J R Hebditch, a Doncaster optician, who in effect saved the house and grounds from ruin. It was purchased by British Ropes in 1960, who built their new head offices in the grounds now occupied (as is the whole site) by the Doncaster Moat House Hotel.

Site: High Road (A630), Warmsworth.

Grid Ref: SE 546004 (Landranger 111, Pathfinder 716)

A Modern Tribute

Next to Conisbrough's library, in a small public garden, can be seen one of South Yorkshire's most dramatic tributes to miners and their wives. The shawled figure of a young woman, hands on hips, looks down in a state of resigned sadness; behind her an almost buried collier, one hand desperately reaching through fallen debris, the other still clutching his coal-face pick.

Executed by Barnsley sculpture Graham Ibbeson, this superb work was commissioned by Doncaster Council (with assistance from arts associations) and placed there in 1987. It commemorates the men and boys who lost their lives at the nearby Denaby and Cadeby collieries *(see page 97)*; and, to quote

from its brass plaque, 'the women who shared their lives and suffered their loss'.

Site: Old Road, Conisbrough town centre.

Grid Ref: SK 510985 (Landranger111, Pathfinder 727)

Summoned by Bell

Built of magnesian limestone rubble on the parson's land, just outside the gates of Warmsworth Hall *(see page 93)*, stands a most unusual belltower. It has a square lower storey — with a boarded entrance door on the south side — and an octagonal upper floor, supporting a wooden open-side cupola with spiked finial.

Difficult to date precisely, the stone part may be late medieval. Its purpose was to announce services and call worshippers to the old St Peter's Church (now gone), which was sited about half a mile (0.8km) away from the village, at the edge of the parish. It may have also come into use to celebrate special events. The tower is an attractive feature set within a pleasant conservation area, despite the proximity of the A1(M).

Site: Warmsworth lies three miles (5km) south-east of Doncaster. The tower is at the junction of Low Road East and Glebe Street, reached via High Road (A630).

Grid Ref: SE 548004 (Landranger 111, Pathfinder 716)

Where Quarrymen Once Lived

A pair of tall abandoned limekilns, set into a bank and with tunnel entrances still visible, is one of the last reminders of Levitt Hagg, a small but thriving community of quarrymen, limeburners and their families.

Limestone was quarried and burnt here from at least the mid-eighteenth century. Peak sales — 23,000 tons — occurred in 1876 when there were twenty-one workers' cottages, two mill-houses plus the mission hall and reading room. Lime was in great demand from the building trade and for industrial processes. The proximity of the River Don and, from 1849, the railway were vital for the development of this specialised community. Stone was carried to the kilns on tramways or hauled in barrows by donkeys. By the 1950s the hamlet was abandoned and cleared, though a large quarry still functions nearby. Today, the old riverside quarry has been transformed — not without controversy — by Yorkshire Environmental as a landfill site.

Site: on east bank of the Don, one mile (1.6km) from Warmsworth and half a mile (0.8km) from Sprotborough Church. Access is on foot: turn off at the hairpin bend of Mill Hill and walk along the trackway for about half a mile (0.8km). Take care as heavy lorries still use the latter part of the route.

Grid Ref: SE 535006 (Landranger 111, Pathfinder 716)

Denaby Main and Jim Macfarlane

A complete colliery winding-wheel marks the landscaped site of Denaby Main Colliery which, when it started coal production in 1868, was the furthest east of any Yorkshire coalmine. A companion pit located a mile (1.6km) away at Cadeby was sunk in 1893, both concerns run by the Denaby and Cadeby Colliery Company. The pits employed over 4,000 men, many of them housed in the company-owned dwellings in the village named after the original colliery.

During the first few decades of operation the miners and their families were subjected to threats and actual eviction whenever industrial disputes arose, culminating in the 'bag-muck strike' of 1902-3. A plaque mounted on the brick base that supports the wheel pays tribute to the 203 men and boys who lost their lives during a century of production, the pit closing in 1968. Another plate pays tribute to Councillor Jim Macfarlane, the university lecturer, leader of Doncaster Council and local historian, who started work at Denaby Main at the age of fourteen and worked tirelessly as an adult educator until his sudden death in 1985. Recent funding success should result in a major sports complex being built near this site.

Site: by the level crossing, just south of the Don on the A6023 Doncaster road between Mexborough and Conisbrough

Grid Ref: SK 493998 (Landranger 111, Pathfinder 727)

Mexborough's Lost 'Castle'

The remains of an artificial mound (or motte) of earth and stone, with surrounding land (or bailey) enclosed by a circular ditch, gave Mexborough the *burgh* element of its place-name. Only a couple of miles from Conisbrough's famous Norman castle, this far less well-known but more ancient feature deserves better recognition.

Writing in the seventeenth century, the respected Yorkshire antiquarian Roger Dodsworth spoke of 'Mexborough where hath once been a castle'. 'Castle Hill' is in fact one of the best surviving examples of a series of defensive hill-top sites in South Yorkshire. Although it does not have the aerial dominance of Bradfield or Laughton-en-le-Morthen, the site was clearly of strategic importance, since it overlooked Stafford Sands, the ancient ford of the River Don where open-air meetings of the Wapentake of Strafforth were held during the period of Danish governance. The archaeology was damaged by landscaping when a public park was created, but despite the steps, paths and flowerbeds, Castle Hill remains an imposing and somewhat mysterious landscape feature.

Site: Castle Hill Park, Doncaster Road, Mexborough (opposite Makin Street).
Grid Ref: SK485999 (Landranger111, Pathfinder 727)

The Site of a Once Thriving Colliery

Fields just west of old Hickleton village, about a mile (1.6km) east of the hamlet of Goldthorpe, were the scene of great activity in 1892 when pit-sinking began, no doubt witnessed by the principal lessor, Viscount Halifax of Hickleton Hall. Some 400 sinkers and workmen were given a celebratory supper by the colliery company, on the 5th July 1894, to mark the 'winning' of the famous Barnsley bed of coal.

Hickleton, with its two deep shafts, was a very modern pit and its successes understandably went hand in hand with the development of the new Dearne towns of Thurnscoe and Goldthorpe. In 1900, 2,552 tons of coal were raised in a day, and annual production soon reached 600,000 tons. Employment peaked in 1931 with a workforce of 4,145. Hickleton Main effectively closed in 1988, like other pits, run down following the 1984/94 strike. When once-great collieries shut down, their distinctive architecture fast disappears through demolition and 'landscaping'. A small modern memorial is virtually all that is left, but recent events such as the Dearne Valley Opera will hopefully remind future generations that there remains much to be celebrated in former South Yorkshire mining communities.

Site: Lidget Lane (B6411 Hickleton–Thunscoe road), by the new Thunscoe Business Park.
Grid Ref: SE 465054 (Landranger Sheet 111, Pathfinder 716)

A Showpiece Shelter Shed

The classical style and extraordinary length (fourteen bays) of this fine arcaded structure is not unlike ranges found by archaeologists on the sites of high-status Roman villas.

It is in fact a nineteenth century shelter shed for farm animals in Italianate style, and probably commisioned by wealthy Charles S A Thellusson of nearby Brodsworth Hall. The round piers, square capitals and segmental arches are made of good-quality limestone under a restored pantile roof. It formed one side of the foldyard of the farm. Within the shelter would have been troughs to serve as mangers and racks to hold the hay. The cattle were protected from the worst of the weather in a convenient place where they could be fed.

Site: about forty yards (35m) north of Manor Farmhouse, Marr, and can be seen from the Barnsley (A635) road.

Grid Ref: SE 517053 (Landranger 111, Pathfinder 716)

A Planned Colliery Village

Brodsworth Main Colliery was sunk between 1905-8 by the Stavely Coal and Iron Company, who quickly established a model village for its employees, based on garden city lines, to the design of architect Percy Houlton.

The houses were built in the fashionable Arts and Crafts style of the period, many with Tudor gables and small-paned windows. A glance at an Ordnance Survey map shows a series of radiating curved avenues linked by more formal straight streets and a core of public buildings. Foremost among them is the brick church of All Saints, conceived by W H Wood in 1914. The tall, slender steeple is a particularly attractive feature and a very distinctive landmark. The mine, once the largest in Britain, closed in 1991.

Site: four miles (6.5km) north-west of Doncaster.

Grid Ref: SE 5308 (Landranger 111, Pathfinder 716)

White Greyhounds

Brodsworth Hall was commissioned by Charles Augustus Thellusson, who had inherited his part of the huge family fortune via the controversial will of his great-grandfather. It was completed between 1861 and 1863, in an Italian classical style to the design of Chevalier Casentini, a somewhat mysterious figure, but re-using some interior features of an earlier, eighteenth century house. Thellusson's artistic taste is further reflected by his collection of marble sculptures, used to enhance the interior.

Casentini also brought over ornaments for the garden, including eight elegant white marble greyhounds, six flanking steps on the terrace of the south or garden front, and two (one of which is illustrated) at the base of the centrally-placed steps to the west (croquet lawn) front. Account books note a consignment in 1867 of 'marble steps and figures and Fountain vase in Pleasure grounds'.

Site: five miles (8km) north-west of Doncaster, with access via Hooton Road (B6422). Open from Easter to the last Sunday in October (not Mondays).

Grid Ref: SE 507071 (Landranger 111, Pathfinder 716)

The Mansion Where Time Stood Still

Brodsworth Hall was given to English Heritage in 1990 by understandably reluctant owners, following the death of Mrs Sylvia Grant-Dalton, a widow who had lived there alone, with the support of a butler, for many years. Most of the original furnishings were intact but required a great deal of specialist attention. The magnesian limestone stonework of the building was suffering from the accumulated effects of acid rain, the huge roof leaked and mining subsidence was evident.

The purchase of the contents, via the National Heritage Fund, marked the beginning of a remarkable process of restoration and especially conservation, prior to public opening in 1995. Today's visitors are not only able to see one of the finest examples of Victorian country-house architecture but also witness the results of countless hours of skillful conservation. The harmful bugs and beetles, and decades of dust and damp, have been halted, but the essential charm of the house retained. Not surprisingly, Brodsworth has won awards and attracts thousands of visitors, but it could very easily have gone the way of many other 'redundant' South Yorkshire mansions.

Site: five miles (8km) north-west of Doncaster, with access via Hooton Road (B6422). Open 1pm–5pm from Easter to the last Sunday in October (not Mondays apart from Bank Holidays).

Grid Ref: SE 507071 (Landranger 111, Pathfinder 716)

A Failed Market

Some Yorkshire communities prospered and developed into thriving centres of trade during the Tudor period, encouraged by the grant of a royal charter for a weekly market;but others, despite such patronage, fell by the wayside.

Hooton Pagnell's market charter was bestowed to Sir Geoffrey Luteral by Henry III in 1253. Such village markets were speculatively created in the thirteenth and fourteenth centuries when trade and population was increasing. Without the necessary presence of entrepreneurship in the form of merchants, shopkeepers and craftsmen, decline was inevitable. Hooton Pagnell was not alone in its demise: not far away, Braithwell, Campsell, Stainforth, Wath and Wortley were also unable to benefit from a royal grant. The remains of the village buttercross at Hooton Pagnell is a relic of late medieval enterprise that failed to materialise in the face of subsequent economic recession. Instead, in the hands of a dominant resident lord, it became a noted estate village.

Site: the village lies almost midway between Barnsley and Doncaster, on the B6422.

Grid Ref: SE 486083 (Land ranger 111, Pathfinder 716)

A Georgian Freezer

Many country houses had an ice-house, often sited near a pond or lake. The ice-house in Howell Wood is a well-preserved example. Its arched entrance leads, via a vaulted passage, through a mound of earth to a typical egg-shaped well about six yards (5.5m) deep. During hard frosts, workers would saw ice from the surface of the nearby pond, packing it in the well between layers of straw. The double brick walls, separated by an air gap, ensured a constant interior temperature. Ice was thus available for domestic use through the summer months, and could in fact be stored for up to three years.

The wood was largely the creation of Barnsley attorney William Marsden, whose Burntwood estate was managed from a small mansion called Burntwood Nook. The ice-house probably served the larger property of Burntwood Hall. Howell Wood Country Park is managed by Doncaster Council's Directorate of Recreation and Cultural Services.

Site: Howell Wood lies about half a mile (0.8km) off the east side of the B6273, between Great Houghton and Brierley Gap crossroads. Access to the car park is via the minor road from Brierley Gap to South Kirkby. Access into the ice-house is by arrangement with the countryside unit/ranger.

Grid Ref: SE 434097 (Landranger 111, Pathfinder 704)

The Deserted Village

By the middle of the seventeenth century all the houses near All Saint's Church, Frickley, had gone, abandoned by its last few inhabitants, leaving the place of worship in complete isolation. The community had always been small — only six married couples and eleven other taxpayers were recorded in 1379. The land here continued to be farmed, using the three village open fields, a generation or more later.

The complete survival of the church may have been due to the patronage of successive squires of Frickley Hall and the needs of worshippers living at nearby Clayton. Later landscaping and farming has destroyed all visual traces of the original settlement, but one wonders what an archaeological investigation might reveal. Until then, Frickley remains an intriguing example of an apparently deserted medieval village.

Site: midway between Clayton and Hooton Pagnell. Access is via a track off Churchfield Road, almost opposite Lodge Farm.

Grid Ref: SE 468079 (Landranger 111, Pathfinder 716)

The Spa that Rivalled Harrogate

During the early 1800s, an increasing number of fashionable visitors were attracted to the spa at Askern, where its 'medicinal waters', according to an 1822 directory, 'both in smell and taste nearly resemble the celebrated waters of Harrogate'. Askern water had one advantage over its fashionable neighbour: it acted as a diuretic, devoid of the 'cathartic power for which the Harrogate waters are so remarkable'. The spring was said to rise from a seven acre (3ha) lake, called Askern Pool, frequented 'by persons afflicted with rheumatic and scorbutic diseases'. Visitors were catered for by an appropriate inn and lodging houses. A week's accommodation at Mr Haigh's establishment cost one guinea, but there was a surcharge of 3d for an hour's ride on the lake pleasure-boat. The 'Old Baths' continued to attract users, as did the new Hydro. John Bigland, author of a visitor's book on Askern, considered the spa to be a pleasant family resort, free of gaming-houses, 'ever select and respectable, from there being no incitements to tempt the visits of needy and rapacious adventurers'.

Site: Askern is about seven miles (11km) north of Doncaster, on the A19. The lake is still an attractive feature.
Grid Ref: SE 563134 (Landranger 111, Pathfinder 704)

Snowdrops at St Mary's

The annual snowdrop festival, held at the end of February or early March, attracts many visitors to the small country churchyard at Kirk Bramwith. Clumps of the dainty white flowers form a natural carpet, brightening the darkest of days.

St Mary's Church has a Norman south doorway and chancel arch, both decorated with scalloped capitals and zigzag carving. Established by the Norman lord Ilbert de Lacey, who had a mighty castle at Pontefract, St Mary's is unusual because of its royal connections. After 1362, Kirk Bramwith — and former de Lacey lands — became the property of John of Gaunt, who was created Duke of Lancaster by his father, King Edward III. Henry Bolingbroke, John's son,was crowned Henry IV in 1399, therefore the living came into royal hands, remaining Crown-controlled until as recently as 1987. Aspects of the later interior of the church reflect this long royal association.

Site: Kirk Bramwith lies about ten miles (16km) north-east of Doncaster, between the New Junction and Stainforth & Keadby canals.

Grid Ref: SE 619118 (Landranger 111, Pathfinder 717)

A Riverside Parish

Windmill, dykes, water meadows and pastures, interesting cottages and a network of green lanes and footpaths — as well as a magnificent church — make up this attractive lowland parish of Fishlake, by the banks of the tidal Don.

The Dutch engineer Cornelius Vermuyden came here in the seventeenth century, having convinced the king that he could drain the land so that it could be used for farming. The Dutchman and his workers were not welcomed by the locals, who were far from pleased with such unnecessary foreign interference. The problem of annual flooding continued into this century until the course of the river was altered and drainage pumps installed.

The church is dedicated to St Cuthbert (his statue in a niche in the west face of the tower), the famous Celtic monk whose much-moved body was believed to have rested here on its way to eventual burial in the cathedral at Durham. St Cuthbert's has a very spacious and light interior, and is mostly late medieval, but its oldest feature is the splendid Norman south door, described by architectural historian Nicholas Pevsner as 'perhaps the most decorated in Yorkshire'.

Site: Fishlake is about seven miles (11km) north-east of Doncaster and two miles (3km) west of Thorne.

Grid Ref: SE 656132 (Landranger 111, Pathfinder 705)

Old Thorne

The Dutch engineer Vermuyden *(see previous page)* lived in Thorne — in the Old Hall, Queen Street — whilst Ashfield Bank was being constructed, part of the drainage and reclamation of marsh and wetlands that began in 1626. The only permanently dry area was a ridge of sand, traversed by a path called High Trod, on which the Norman motte and bailey castle and parish church were built.

William de Warenne, the Norman overlord of Thorne and builder of Conisbrough Castle *(see page 96)*, fortified Peel Hill with stone transported via the Don from Sprotbrough. The Norman parish church of St Nicholas was rebuilt in the fourteenth and fifteenth centuries. Leland provides us with an impression of the area in 1538: 'By the Church Garth of Thurne is a praty pile or castlet well diked and now used for offenders in the forests ...'. Poachers were imprisoned for taking game from the royal forest of Hatfield Chase, of which Thorne was a part. Thorne was granted a market charter in 1658, renewed by Charles II with the addition of two annual fairs, held in June and October. Despite erosion by mountain bikes, the motte and its now-dry circular moat is an important reminder of Thorne's medieval origins, and deserves better respect.

Site: Church Street and Peel Hill.

Grid Ref: SK 689132 (Landranger 111/112, Pathfinder 705)

Further Reading

D Ashurst, *The History of South Yorkshire Glass*, J R Collis, 1994.

D Bayliss (ed), *A Guide to the Industrial History of South Yorkshire,* Association of Industrial Archaeology, 1995.

T W Beastall, *Tickhill: Portrait of an English Country Town,* Waterdale Press, 1995.

F Bottomley, *Yorkshire Churches*, Alan Sutton, 1993.

Brodsworth Hall, English Heritage, 1995.

B Elliott (ed), *Aspects of Barnsley*, vols 1-4, Wharncliffe Publishing, 1993-6.

B Elliott, *The Making of Barnsley*, Wharncliffe Publishing, 1988.

B Elliott (ed), *Aspects of Doncaster*, Wharncliffe Publishing, 1997.

D Hey, *The Making of South Yorkshire*, Moorland Publishing, 1979.

D Hey, *Packmen, Carriers and Packhorse Roads*, Leicester University Press, 1980.

D Hey, *Buildings of Britain, 1550-1750: Yorkshire*, Moorland Publishing, 1981.

D Hey, M Olive & M Liddament, *Forging the Valley*, Sheffield Academic Press, 1997.

J Hunter, *South Yorkshire* (2 vols), 1828-31.

M Jones (ed), *Aspects of Rotherham*, vols 1-2, Wharncliffe Publishing, 1995-6.

M Jones (ed), *Aspects of Sheffield*, Wharncliffe Publishing, 1997.

A Munford, *Rotherham: A Pictorial History*, Phillimore, 1994.

P F Ryder, *Medieval Buildings of Yorkshire*, Ash Grove Books, 1992.

D & T Smith, *South & West Yorkshire Curiosities*, Dovecote Press, 1992.

H Smith, *A History of Rotherham's Roads and Transport*, Rotherham Libraries, 1992.

Index